OPENING C

A Word from the Editing Room... 2

Remembering Sally Kellerman... 3

In Memoriam... 4

Killer Cop by Joe Secrett... 5

Names is for Tombstones, Baby - 007 Takes on Black Power in Live and Let Die by John Harrison... 8

The Owl and the Pussycat by Rachel Bellwoar... 16

To Be Savage, Hungry and Free by Allen Rubinstein... 19

Star Trek: The Motion Picture - Boldly Going Where the TV Show Had Gone Before by Martin Dallard... 27

A Deep Dive into Deep End by David Michael Brown... 32

Jane Asher Talks Deep End... 36

Re-Inventing the Past - Hollywood Celebrates Itself by Brian J. Robb..... 39

A Clockwork Orange is a Rite of Passage by Sebastian Corbascio........... 48

The Muppet Movie by Kevin Nickelson... 54

Two-Minute Warning by Darren Linder... 57

Ulzana's Raid - A Bloody Masterpiece by James Lecky... 62

Pond Scum of the Earth - Remembering Frogs by Steven West............... 66

Jane Fonda in the '70s by John H. Foote... 71

Tam Lin by Simon J. Ballard... 79

Hustle by Dr. Andrew C. Webber... 83

I Never Miss a Liv Ullman Musical - Lost Horizon by Peter Sawford....... 86

Adventures of a Second Division Sex Pest by Ian Taylor... 91

Original Artwork by the Students of Confetti Institute of Creative Technologies... 97

Closing Credits... 99

Contributors this issue: Simon J. Ballard, Rachel Bellwoar, David Michael Brown, Sebastian Corbascio, Martin Dallard, John H. Foote, John Harrison, James Lecky, Darren Linder, Kevin Nickelson, Brian J. Robb, Allen Rubinstein, Peter Sawford, Joe Secrett, Ian Taylor, Dr Andrew C. Webber, Steven West. Caricature artwork by Aaron Stielstra.

All articles, photographs and specially produced artwork remain copyright their respective author/photographer/artist. Opinions expressed herein are those of the individual.

Design and Layout: Dawn Dabell
Copy Editor: Jonathon Dabell

Most images in this magazine come from the private collection of Dawn and Jonathon Dabell, or the writer of the corresponding article. Those which do not are made available in an effort to advance understanding of cultural issues pertaining to academic research. We believe this constitutes 'fair use' of any such copyrighted material as provided for in Section 107 of the US Copyright Law. In accordance with Title U.S.C Section 107, this magazine is sold to those who have expressed a prior interest in receiving the included information for research, academic and educational purposes.

Printed globally by Amazon KDP

A Word from the Editing Room

Salutations, '70s movie lovers!

Welcome to Issue 6 of 'Cinema of the '70s'. We're delighted to offer another eclectic smorgasbord of content in this latest edition, including the cover piece by John Harrison about the James Bond film *Live and Let Die* (1973), Darren Linder's excellent examination of *Two-Minute Warning* (1976), Martin Dallard taking a look at *Star Trek: The Motion Picture* (1979), John H. Foote's exhaustive overview of Jane Fonda's '70s movies and an exclusive interview with Jane Asher, who speaks to David Michael Brown about her work on the cult gem *Deep End* (1970). We also extend a warm welcome to our newest writer, Sebastian Corbascio, who casts his eye over Stanley Kubrick's controversial classic *A Clockwork Orange* (1971).

We dedicate this issue to Joseph Parra, a stage actor and huge supporter of independent print projects such as this magazine; more importantly, a close friend of many of our contributing writers and readers. Joseph passed away earlier in the year at the age of 68, taken too young by cancer. His energy, positivity and enthusiasm for all things stage-and-screen-related will be sorely missed.

Such has been the success and positive buzz surrounding this '70s-themed publication that we have been persuaded to launch a sister mag which focuses on '80s movies. Look out for 'Cinema of the '80s' Issue 1, which will be making an appearance in the coming months.

In the meantime, enjoy the latest issue. And we hope to see you back for Issue 7 when the time comes.

Dawn and Jonathon Dabell

Remembering Sally Kellerman (1937-2022)

Sally Kellerman passed away on February 24th, 2022, in Woodland Hills, Los Angeles. She died as a result of heart failure at a care facility where she had been residing since being diagnosed with dementia. She was 84.

Kellerman was particularly prominent on '70s cinema screens. She shot to stardom at the start of decade, appearing as Major Margaret 'Hot Lips' Houlihan in Robert Altman's iconic *M*A*S*H* (1970), a performance which garnered her one and only Oscar nomination. It was a career-defining role, and remains arguably the first to spring to mind whenever her name is mentioned. Famously, she turned down the role of Linda Rogo in *The Poseidon Adventure* (1972), which eventually went to Stella Stevens.

Kellerman's '70s film credits were:
M*A*S*H (1970)
Brewster McCloud (1970)
Last of the Red Hot Lovers (1972)
A Reflection of Fear (1972)
Slither (1973)
Lost Horizon (1973)
Rafferty and the Gold Dust Twins (1975)
The Big Bus (1976)
Welcome to L.A. (1976)
The Mouse and His Child (1977)
A Little Romance (1979)

Goodbye, Miss Kellerman. Sleep well and thanks for the memories.
RIP

In Memoriam

**David Birney
(1939-2022)**
Actor, known for *Caravan to Vaccares* (1974) and *Trial by Combat* (1976).

**Veronica Carlson
(1944-2022)**
Actress, known for *The Horror of Frankenstein* (1970) and *The Ghoul* (1975).

**Howard Hesseman
(1940-2022)**
Actor, known for *The Big Bus* (1976) and *Americathon* (1979).

**Hardy Kruger
(1928-2022)**
Actor, known for *A Bridge Too Far* (1977) and *The Wild Geese* (1978).

**James Olson
(1930-2022)**
Actor, known for *Crescendo* (1970) and *The Andromeda Strain* (1971).

**Nehemiah Persoff
(1919-2022)**
Actor, known for *Mrs Pollifax-Spy* (1971) and *Voyage of the Damned* (1976).

**Mitchell Ryan
(1934-2022)**
Actor, known for *High Plains Drifter* (1973) and *Magnum Force* (1973).

**Fred Ward
(1942-2022)**
Actor, known for *Tilt* (1979) and *Escape from Alcatraz* (1979).

**Dennis Waterman
(1948-2022)**
Actor, known for *Scars of Dracula* (1970) and *Sweeney!* (1977).

**Jimmy Wang Yu
(1943-2022)**
Actor, known for *The Man from Hong Kong* (1973) and *One-Armed Boxer II* (1976).

Killer Cop

by Joe Secrett

'70s Italy was a highly political and literal warzone. With the Red Brigade committing acts of bombing, kidnapping and assassination, it seemed like there would be no end to the turmoil. Crime in general was rampant, and there were times when it felt like it would never calm down. Directors, writers and actors in the country often reflected these incidents in their movies, depicting law enforcers battling against terrorism, corruption and extortion. *Killer Cop* (1975) is one such example of this 'Eurocrime' genre (or 'poliziotteschi'). It manages to utilise most of these ideas, taking as its basis - at least partially - a true incident that had taken place a few years earlier.

Cinemagoers at the time wanted to see criminals and corrupt characters getting their just desserts. They craved tough cops who were happy to bend the rules to achieve violent justice. They wanted these cops to prevail against the completely ruthless criminal minds. An actor named Maurizio Merli enjoyed particular success with this formula, his characters adopting a shoot-first, beat-up-and-interrogate-later style which proved a hit with audiences. Many of his films could be seen as gonzo, violence-laden crime epics (not that there's anything wrong with that). But there were other films in the genre (like *Killer Cop*,

which didn't feature Merli) which found other ways of providing thrilling tales of good (sometimes) triumphing over evil, or in some cases, exposing the truth. Over-the-top gunplay and nudity weren't always necessary.

Killer Cop - or, to use its Italian name, *La Polizia ha le mani legate* - is a 1975 production based loosely on a real bombing incident which had taken place in 1969. The Piazza Fontana bombing occurred in a bank in Milan, killing 17 and seriously wounding 88 people. The film's premise changes slightly - instead of a bank being targeted, it's a hotel.

Cop Matteo Rolandi (the late, great Claudio Cassinelli) witnesses the blast while working on an unrelated drugs case, and finds himself driven to find the culprit. A key suspect is Ludovisi (Bruno Zanin), but all the while a shady organisation is pulling strings to make sure Rolandi's leads are silenced. He faces challenges too from his superiors, one such being the prosecutor Armando Di Federico (Arthur Kennedy). This story is as much about wading through red tape and petty police politics as it is about actually solving a crime. Kennedy shines in his role (he dubbed himself in the English language version, which helps greatly), and proves a fine foil for Cassinelli. Di

Federico trusts policemen very little and trying to keep Rolandi under control causes him stress aplenty, leading to some memorable exchanges.

Armando and Rolandi butt heads repeatedly during the investigation, with Rolandi's good friend and partner Luigi (Franco Fabrizi) on hand to provide a touch of relief with his mildly comical nature and fidgety mannerisms (like having a quick sip of Rolandi's coffee before he brings it into his office). Kennedy was part of a slew of American/British/European stars who sought work abroad, sometimes due to their waning careers, sometimes for a change of pace, or sometimes merely to collect a quick paycheck and a holiday. Other stars did it frequently, including Jack Palance, Richard Conte, Lee J. Cobb, James Mason and Farley Granger, to name a few. Even a young Tom Skerritt did it, appearing in *Run, Run, Joe!* in 1974.

Unlike other Eurocrime outings, *Killer Cop* sets aside a meaty chunk of its running time to flesh out the main protagonists and antagonists. This helps paint the bigger picture of all the people involved. Rolandi and his partner provide comic foil for each other; Di Federico is all business; the bomber Ludovisi and his partners in crime scramble to figure out their next move from their hidden employers. Zanin plays Ludovisi as a scared, timid man. Despite having committed a major act of violence, he seems to be losing his mind as he is slowly betrayed by his bosses. This causes him to become paranoid and crazy, leading to more perilous situations. A great example of this shows him visiting an optician after his glasses are lost during the explosion. He eventually makes off wearing the test glasses, which he wears for the remainder of the film! He's not committed to the cause, just a lowly foot soldier who is abandoned and left to his own devices when the initial plan spirals out of control. Zanin almost makes us feel a sense of pity towards the poor Ludovsi. When you consider what he's done and how he carries himself, you realise the character hasn't been right in the head from the start.

Even the members of the 'Hidden Organisation' are given limited screen time, often seen well-dressed in suits in a very '70s lounge, giving orders over a telephone to a hired killer played by spaghetti western and Eurocrime regular Giovanni Cianfriglia. Cianfriglia was an actor and a stuntman during his varied career and made a killing (pun intended) playing villains, hitmen and - very rarely - good guys in a variety of westerns, crime dramas and comedies in the '60s, '70s and '80s. Whenever you see his name in the cast, it's usually a safe bet there's going to be violence and action and people are going to die during the course of the story! As of writing this, he is still going strong at the age of 87.

Like all good conspiracy thrillers, *Killer Cop* has characters with ulterior motives and creates questions for our intrepid policeman to answer. Why does the prosecutor want to keep a tight lid on the proceedings, for example? Why do suspects and even officers of the law end up being bumped off? Why do leads turn out to be dead ends? It all culminates in a rather frantic and wild shootout in a subway which answers few questions and raises many, many more. Corruption in the police force was a very realistic threat back then. This background really helps keep the pace moving, as Rolandi begins his descent into the depraved world of suspected terrorism, murders and seedy organisations. More than once, his trust in his fellow officers is brought into question. Stelvio Cipriani provides a mellow yet moody soundtrack which keeps things ticking along steadily. He uses the main theme throughout, breaking it up and slowing it down in different reprisals which really help the tense atmosphere.

The symbolism could not be more obvious, as Cassinelli's cop reads a copy of 'Moby Dick'. This links neatly with the idea of a man going up against a great beast (in this case, an unknown but very powerful political 'giant' which he hopes to bring down against his superior's orders). Cassinelli is fantastic as the curious and quick-witted Rolandi. He played both sides of the law throughout his career and was equally adept portraying a cop or a criminal. One of his best 'bad guy' roles was in *Milano Violenta* aka *Bloody Payroll* (1976) alongside the tall and gaunt John Steiner.

Sadly, tragedy would strike in the mid '80s while Cassinelli was working on a film in America. On Friday, 12th July, 1985, he and a pilot named Dennis Nasca were killed while filming *Hands of Steel*. Their helicopter struck part of the structure of the Navajo Bridge, causing the helicopter to crash 500 feet into the Colorado River below. He was only 46 years old. Cassinelli left behind a great legacy of films, most of which have large cult followings and attract regular viewers to this day. He even appeared in some international productions, like the underrated *Avalanche Express*, as well as working with Bond girl Barbara Bach in *The Great Alligator* and *Island of the Fishmen* (all 1979), and many more.

Killer Cop is a fan favourite in its genre. It has all the ingredients of a good police thriller, and is peppered with great performances throughout. Though not as nasty and sleazy as other outings, it still has some minor violence. The rough stuff is more shocking when it eventually happens because you're not really expecting it. *Killer Cop* proves a tense, well-written outing which, for the uninitiated, makes a great introduction to the Eurocrime genre.

LA P.A.C. PRESENTA CLAUDIO CASSINELLI • ARTHUR KENNEDY IN

LA POLIZIA HA LE MANI LEGATE

CON SARA SPERATI • FRANCO FABRIZI • BRUNO ZANIN REGIA DI LUCIANO ERCOLI

DIRETTORE DELLA FOTOGRAFIA MARCELLO GATTI   MUSICHE DI STELVIO CIPRIANI   UNA PRODUZIONE P.A.C.   REALIZZATA DA ALBERTO PUGLIESE LUCIANO ERCOLI

TECHNICOLOR

NAMES IS FOR TOMBSTONES, BABY

007 TAKES ON BLACK POWER IN LIVE AND LET DIE

by John Harrison

The early '70s was a very tumultuous and transitional, not to mention uncertain, time for the cultural phenomenon that is James Bond 007. As a popular literary figure, Ian Fleming's suave super-spy had been thrilling readers for nearly twenty years, while as a cinematic juggernaut, the character was fast approaching its ten-year anniversary. Fleming had died in 1964, so he was not going to be around to pound out endless novels for the filmmakers to adapt. Though the books and their cinematic adaptations rarely shared much beyond the title, and the name of a character or two, it was still important to have an official Fleming title attached to a movie.

While Bond had enjoyed an incredible five-year run at the cinemas between 1962-1967, anchored of course by the impossibly charismatic Sean Connery in the lead role, the films had started to become a victim of their own success. The productions became massive, the plots more grand and fantastical, and the character became a merchandising giant, as well as the epitome of '60s swagger and cool. When Connery walked away from the role following *You Only Live Twice* (1967), the films continued with unknown Australian model George Lazenby playing Bond in *On Her Majesty's Secret Service* (1969). While that movie would actually turn out to be one of the strongest and most interesting of the entire series (and still a top five Bond to this date), audiences found it tough to accept another actor in the role after

Connery, and Lazenby's performance came in for a lot of criticism. Connery was always going to be a hard act to follow, and Lazenby's lack of acting experience makes itself obvious, but he still managed to be debonair and charming, and looked cut from a similar physical mould as Connery. And it helped that he was surrounded by a fine cast that included Telly Savalas and Diana Rigg. *On Her Majesty's Secret Service* made money, but its box-office returns were not as strong as the previous few Connery movies. Contrary to popular rumours that circled at the time, producers Albert R. "Cubby" Broccoli and Harry Saltzman were prepared to stick with Lazenby in the hope he would grow into the role. It was Lazenby himself who effectively let himself be talked out of continuing the role by his manager, who was convinced Bond would become an archaic stereotype and laughingstock if they tried to bring the character into the '70s.

With a then-enormous, lucrative sum of US $1.25 million offered to him, along with starring roles in two further United Artists productions of his choice, Connery was lured back for *Diamonds are Forever* (1971), the first Bond to be released in the new decade. *Diamonds are Forever* is certainly enjoyable, and those sequences capturing the Las Vegas of its era become increasingly stunning as the years pass and that era continues to fade. It also performed significantly better financially that *On Her Majesty's Secret Service*, despite being by far the lesser film of the two. But it was clearly just a desperate stop-gap measure for the franchise. Using his salary for the film to establish the Scottish International Education Trust, Connery, as charismatic as ever but clearly starting to look a little aged and haggard in *Diamonds are Forever*, made it quite clear that he was now done. The producers' decision to try and cast an unknown who had some physical resemblance to Connery had not worked out, so the hunt was on for the best name actor they could find to fill 007's lofty shoes. Names like Burt Reynolds, John Gavin and even Adam West (!) were approached, before it was decided that James Bond should never be played by an American. Jon Finch, hot off Polanski's *Macbeth* (1971) and Hitchcock's *Frenzy* (1972), was offered the role but turned it down, before it ultimately went to Roger Moore. Moore, who had already proven himself adept at playing suave spy Simon Templar on television's *The Saint* (1962-1969), had already found himself in the consideration mix for both the first Bond feature, *Dr. No* (1962), and *On Her Majesty's Secret Service*.

While it's irresistible to ponder what Finch may have brought to the role had he taken it, Moore would prove to be the perfect choice to inhabit Bond for that era. Forty-five at the time of his casting, Moore was actually older than Connery by nearly three years but looked much younger. Moore was handsome and clean-cut but imbued with boyish cheek. He was also perennially tanned, had perfect hair and a good physique, and looked great in both a tuxedo and a safari suit. While *Diamonds are Forever* had a pervading air of '60s hangover, Moore's James Bond was a distinctly '70s man, and no one could raise a concerned eyebrow better than him. He was softer looking in the face than Connery, which actually made his Bond come across as a lot crueller when he needed to be (such as those moments when he was forced to get tough with the opposite sex).

Broccoli and Saltzman had already settled on *Live and Let Die* as the next film during production of *Diamonds are Forever*. Tom Mankiewicz, who co-wrote *Diamonds are Forever* with Richard Maibaum, began writing the screenplay for *Live and Let Die* in the hope that Connery might still come back. When it became clear that wasn't going to happen, and the series was going to have to reset with a new lead, it was decided to stick with the original plan to adapt *Live and Let Die*, with Mankiewicz fine-tuning his script to make it more reflective of Moore's acting style and interpretation of the material.

Fleming's original novel (the second in his Bond adventures, first published in 1954) saw Bond being sent to New York to investigate 'Mr. Big', a notorious criminal thought to be smuggling British 17th century gold coins into the US via Jamaica. By the early '70s, however, gold coins would have been a bit too low-key and passe when it came to exciting audiences. Drugs were a lot more

intriguing and dangerous, not to mention profitable, so Mankiewicz reinvented Mr. Big as a heroin importer, who plans to flood New York with two tonnes of free heroin brought in from the Caribbean, in a scheme to put all the rival drug lords out of business, so he can then move in and claim the monopoly. In order to help his scheme succeed, Mr. Big relies on the remarkable psychic intuitions of the beautiful and virginal Solitaire whom the crime boss keeps under very close guard. Mr. Big also has the protection of Dr. Kananga, the corrupt Prime Minister of San Monique, the Caribbean island on which his heroin-producing poppy fields are growing, protected from nosey locals by the spectre of voodoo and the occult. When 007 is sent to investigate after a number of his fellow agents

turn up dead, Bond seduces Solitaire and enlists her aid in taking down both Mr. Big and Dr. Kananga, who end up being a lot closer related than first thought.

One of Mankiewicz's prime reasons for wanting to adapt *Live and Let Die* is that he saw it as the perfect opportunity for a Bond film to align itself with the Black Power movement of the day, which was making itself prominent both on the streets and in the arts. This was also the time of the blaxploitation films, a genre which enjoyed a few years of popularity in the wake of movies like *Cotton Comes to Harlem* (1970), *Sweet Sweetback's Baadasssss Song* (1971) and *Shaft* (1971). Usually urban-set, pumping with funky soundtracks, and featuring outsiders and criminals as their anti-heroes, the blaxploitation films found appeal well outside the Black American audiences they were primarily aimed at, prompting mainstream movies from the big studios to incorporate some of the elements of the genre in their own productions, with *Live and Let Die* being a perfect example. Given the film's subject matter and characters, and the time in which it was produced, the depiction of race is an important element of *Live and Let Die*. While there is a lot of racism inherent in Fleming's novel, particularly in the dialogue used to describe the African American dialect, the film keeps things as pretty much expected for the blaxploitation era. All of the criminals in the movie are black, including beautiful double agent Rosie Carver (Gloria Hendry), who becomes the traditional sacrificial lamb, killed after falling for Bond's charms. Many of the black characters are portrayed as being

very fearful of voodoo, and of course Mr. Big and his main henchmen like to dress in the flashy, fly style of the day.

Just as stereotypical, if not even more so, is the character of J. W. Pepper (Clifton James), the slobby Louisiana sheriff who gets mixed-up in a high-speed boat chase across the bayous between Bond and some of Mr. Big's men. Southern-set action flicks were starting to gain traction in the early '70s, thanks to movies like *Deliverance* (1972) and *White Lightning* (1973), both starring Burt Reynolds, who would also later star in the genre-defining *Smokey and the Bandit* (1977). Overweight, bumbling, with a thick Southern drawl, J. W. Pepper is just the kind of inept sheriff who would often populate the more comical Southern action movies, not to mention on episodic TV shows, most notably the popular *Dukes of Hazzard* (1979-1985). While he may have been funny to a ten-year-old kid, J. W. Pepper is a pretty annoying character, a one-note joke that is stretched out far too long. He was obviously popular in the day, though, as he would make an unwelcome return in the next Bond film, *The Man with the Golden Gun* (1974).

Along with its blaxploitation elements, *Live and Let Die* also flirts with the horror genre, as reflected in its black magic subplot, and the incorporation of it throughout the film, but especially during the climax, which takes place during a voodoo sacrifice on the fictional island of San Monique, where Solitaire is to be the intended offering. The character of Baron Samedi, a towering figure who works for Mr. Big and also plays the part of a voodoo high priest in a flashy dance act for San Monique tourists, also lends the film an air of the supernatural. Played with a maniacal laugh and great physical presence by the statuesque Geoffrey Holder, Baron Samedi is a very imposing and frightening character, and while Bond ultimately dispatches him with some ease, the memorable final shot of the film seems to suggest that he has s u r v i v e d, or been reincarnated, which again accentuates the horror elements. To

helm *Live and Let Die*, the producers brought back Guy Hamilton, who had directed the uneven *Diamonds are Forever*, but had also delivered the superb *Goldfinger* (1964), so his Bond cred was still pretty solid. With filming taking place in New York, Jamaica and Louisiana, along with interiors at Pinewood Studios back in England, it's fair to say Hamilton delivered a movie which split the middle between his two previous outings. He handles the action scenes well, even if they do go on a bit long, and the New York scenes are terrific. It's something of a pity that more of the film was not shot there, but of course Bond films need to serve as exotic travelogues. The Louisiana scenes, filmed in New Orleans' infamous French Quarter as well as out on the bayous, also capture the unique locations well, giving a new and different visual spin to a Bond movie. There is also the great crocodile sequence, which again helps to highlight the film's horror elements, and was filmed at a place called the Jamaica Safari Village ("Trespasses Will Be Eaten"). The place was run by a man named Ross Kananga, a moniker screenwriter

Mankiewicz liked so much he stole it for his villain.

While landing the coveted role of the new James Bond girl would guarantee the actress chosen a moment of instant worldwide fame, what it didn't guarantee was longevity. Thankfully, Jane Seymour turned out to be one of the luckier ones, and she imbues Solitaire with an ethereal beauty and innocence, but also has a bit of a cheeky, knowing gleam in her eyes. Costume designer Julie Harris also wraps her in some beautifully opulent and colourful   gowns which emphasize her psychic abilities. While Solitaire   in the novel had the power of second sight, her use of a tarot card deck was something introduced for the film, and it's another element which adds to its '70s vibe, reflecting the New Age beliefs that were   emerging in the wake of the counterculture. The tarot cards also gave artist Robert McGinnis something unique and colourful to work with when it came time to designing the poster art for *Live and Let Die*.

Cast in the dual roles of Dr. Kananga and Mr. Big, Yaphet Kotto exudes a lot of quiet but powerful dignity as the former, and a violent force of nature as the second (a character he achieves with the use of some clever prosthetics and an afro wig). After several years of bit parts and appearances on episodic TV shows, Kotto at the time was starting to come into his own as an actor, after lead turns in *Bone* (1972) and the brilliant crime classic *Across 110th Street* (1972). Dr. Kananga/Mr. Big may not be the most memorable of Bond villains, but the double identity angle is intriguing, and it's a lot of fun to watch Kotto in the dual roles, clearly relishing the opportunity. It's also refreshing to see Bond going up against a main villain who is young and energetic, and physically powerful (at 33, Kotto was the youngest Bond baddie to date).

Of the regular supporting players, *Live and Let Die* sees the return of both Bernard Lee as M, and Lois Maxwell as Miss Moneypenny, though Desmond Llewelyn's Q character is conspicuously absent. Llewelyn was apparently ready to take time off from his television program, *Follyfoot*, to join the production, but it was eventually decided to keep Q out of the film altogether, fearing the series was becoming too focused and reliant on gadgets over story. Hammer fans will enjoy seeing Madeline Smith as an Italian spy with whom Bond is having a post-mission dalliance at the start of the movie, and Julius Harris as the villainous Tee Hee makes for a formidable henchman. With his mechanical, pincer-tipped metal arm (replacing the one a crocodile took from him years earlier), Tee Hee is something of a template for Richard Kiel's Jaws character, who would find enormous favour a couple of films down the track.

One of the finer new additions to the cast of *Live and Let Die* is David Hedison as Felix Leiter, Bond's American friend and colleague in the CIA. Hedison was the fifth actor to play Leiter in as many film appearances, but the first to really bring any genuine charisma to the role (though I do also love the way Jack Lord portrayed him in *Dr. No*). With his distinctive voice and handsome, swarthy features, Hedison found favour with genre fans thanks to his starring role in *The Fly* (1958), and on Irwin Allen's sci-fi/adventure television series *Voyage to the Bottom of the Sea* (1964-1968), and he puts his talents to great use as Leiter, allowing the character to finally be imbued with a bit of genuine personality. It's a pity Leiter did not appear in any of the future Roger Moore films, though Hedison did make a welcome return to the character in *Licence to Kill* (1989), which seemed appropriate since that film lifted Leiter's shark mauling moment from the *Live and Let Die* novel ("He disagreed with something that ate him"). Another major moment from the novel which was not used in the film adaptation, but was later cherry-picked and used in *For Your Eyes Only* (1981), is its climax, where Mr. Big drags Bond and Solitaire at high speed across a jagged coral reef, ripping their skin open to attract the local sharks.

To further emphasize that this was a new Bond geared to the '70s, the producers went for a more modern, pop-oriented flavour for its soundtrack, bringing in George Martin to compose the score. Martin, of course, was well-known and acclaimed for his ground-breaking work producing the Beatles throughout their career. Martin had previously produced the classic Shirley Bassey theme song for *Goldfinger* (1964), but this would be his first time composing the actual score for a Bond movie, and it represented something of a bold move for the producers, who had used the reliable John Barry on all previous films.

Martin would also produce the all-important theme song, which was composed by Paul and Linda McCartney, and performed by Paul McCartney and Wings. While his post-Beatles career had gotten off to an inconsistent start, there were few bigger pop stars in the world at the time than McCartney, and his theme for *Live and Let Die* became a huge chartbuster, and the biggest Bond hit so far, going top ten in most countries, and

reaching No. 2 in the United States. With its quiet, piano intro leading into a raucous explosion of brass, keyboards, pumping bass and odd sound effects, the song marked a radical departure from the more traditional style of the previous Bond themes. While they started flirting with the idea with Nancy Sinatra's theme song for *You Only Live Twice*, *Live and Let Die* finally saw the Bond producers embracing a more pop-rock approach for their title tunes, something they would return to frequently for future films. McCartney recorded the *Live and Let Die* theme in October of 1972 at AIR Studios in London, during sessions for the *Red Rose Speedway* album. While we sadly never got to see the Fab Four themselves do a theme song for one of the '60s Bond films, the soundtrack to *Live and Let Die* gives us the next best thing. Today, the song endures as one of McCartney and Wings' most popular, and remains a highlight of McCartney's live shows. It was also the first Bond theme to be nominated for an Academy Award, but lost out to *The Way We Were*. A more soulful, nightclub-funky version of the song also features in the film, performed by female American singer B. J. Arnau in one of the scenes inside the Fillet of Soul restaurant.

To accompany the theme song, Maurice Binder came up with one of his most visually arresting opening title sequences, which beautifully plays on the film's occult and voodoo elements. Featuring nude African-American women against dark backdrops, illuminated only by a bit of coloured gel lighting and streaks of red flame, the title sequence would not look out of place in one of the blaxploitation horror movies of the day. Binder also pairs the images quite dynamically with the tempo of the song,

a lovely female face immediately turning into a flame-engulfed skull the moment the full bombast of the song kicks in.

One name featured in the credits for *Live and Let Die* that will be of interest to fans of low-budget, regional genre filmmaking is that of William Grefé, who was responsible for capturing the shark footage. The Florida-based Grefé was the director (and sometimes writer) of a number of uniquely bizarre exploitation flicks lensed in that state, including *Sting of Death* (1966), *Death Curse of Tartu* (1966), *The Wild Rebels* (1967), *Stanley* (1972) and *Mako: The Jaws of Death* (1976).

Ultimately, when looked at as a part of the overall series, *Live and Let Die* ranks amongst the rung of second-tier Bond films. It does have something of a unique feel compared to the others, in that it almost seems more akin to a Bond rip-off than a genuine Bond film. It's Roger Corman-esque flavour is compounded by the first use of a four-letter word in a Bond film ("Holy shit", uttered by Mrs. Bell, the incredulous flying student, after Bond takes her on a winged demolition derby through a small airport). But the movie's value as a piece of Saturday afternoon matinee entertainment is undeniable, and while critical reception was mixed, the box-office was excellent. Moore didn't really come in to his own as 007 until the magnificent *The Spy Who Loved Me* (1977), but *Live and Let Die* provided ample encouragement that the Bond franchise did not have to be anchored to one actor or one decade to succeed. If done right, the appeal is timeless. The decade that followed *Live and Let Die* proved that Roger Moore was the best, and right, choice for the role, even if he did stick around for one or two films too many.

To coincide with the release of *Live and Let Die*, Pan not only published the customary paperback tie-in edition of Fleming's novel, but also issued a companion paperback titled 'Roger Moore as James Bond'. Presented as a personal diary of Moore's first-hand account of filming the movie, and containing eight pages of colour photographs, the actor may have had some assistance in writing the book, or at least gave it some decent polishing prior to publication, but his distinct personality does come across well in the prose, making it a genuinely enjoyable read. It also provides a very interesting look into the production, and the relationship between Roger and his producers, director and co-stars. Mass market 'Making Of' movie paperbacks became an increasingly regular thing on the shelves as the '70s progressed, and 'Roger Moore as James Bond' was one of the more unique ones. It remained out of print for many years, before finally being reissued in a hardcover edition by The History Press in 2018, in time for the film's 45th anniversary.

The merchandising of James Bond had slowed down somewhat since the heady days of the mid '60s, resulting in very few original tie-ins for *Live and Let Die*, apart from the two paperbacks and the usual soundtrack LP. There were a couple of interesting exceptions, though. One was the *Live and Let Die* Viewmaster set of 3D reels, the first of only two Bond films to get the Viewmaster treatment (1979's *Moonraker* being the other). The other, more exotic item was the James Bond 007 Tarot Game, which came with a deck of tarot cards, featuring the illustrations Fergus Hall painted for the film, and a fold-out instructional booklet and poster sheet. As an interesting piece of trivia, Salvador Dalí was originally approached to paint the cards, however his fee was too much for even a Bond budget to afford. Dalí would eventually release his own tarot cards in 1984, inspired perhaps by his initial approach to work on the film.

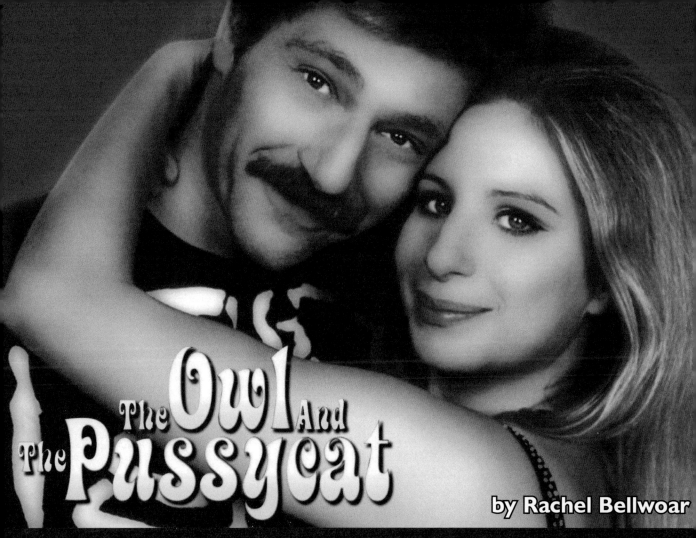

The Owl And The Pussycat

by Rachel Bellwoar

Herbert Ross' *The Owl and the Pussycat* might share its title with an Edward Lear poem, but it's Bill Manhoff's play that serves as the source material. Originally staged on Broadway in the '60s, with Alan Alda and Diana Sands as the leads, Ross' film casts George Segal and Barbra Streisand (in her first non-musical film) in the roles.

The first big difference between the film and the play is the setting. Segal and Streisand were both native New Yorkers (still, in Streisand's case) and the film moves the action from San Francisco to New York. Not that San Francisco made much of an impression in the Broadway production. On stage, Felix and Doris were restricted to Felix's apartment. Time passes but every scene takes place in that apartment. In the screen version, Ross opens things out and allows the characters to walk and talk around the city, using real locations to generate an authentic, on-the-go feel.

Manhoff's play begins with Doris knocking on Felix's door. Buck Henry (who would go on to be the co-writer of another Streisand vehicle, *What's Up, Doc?*) wrote the screenplay adaptation, and gives Doris (Streisand) and Felix (Segal) their own character introductions.

First, we meet Doris. A newspaper doesn't offer much defense against rain, but it's all she has in the opening scene, which shows the harshness of New York, cars honking as Doris tries to cross the street. Stopping in the doorway of a store for a moment to get some cover, she puts on her sunglasses (despite it being dark out) and then joins the line for the bus. Just as she's about to board, the bus driver closes the door in her face. Was the bus full? Did the driver judge her for what she was wearing (a fuzzy coat that leaves her legs bare)? Whatever the reason, Doris is stuck in the rain once more, which is when the film gives viewers their first taste of her interior monologue. Ross only uses this device twice, and never with Felix. It's also worth noting that the two scenes involving an interior monologue are very similar, in that they both show moments when she has to decide whether or not she's going to accept a man's help, knowing that he might expect sex in return. In this instance, Doris decides to accept a ride home from a stranger and, sure enough, instead of dropping her off and pulling away, the man gets out of the car and follows her inside.

What we learn about Doris from hearing her interior monologue in this scene is that, despite all of these things happening to her - the bus, the creepy man, etc. - she isn't

called the landlord. It doesn't matter that the only reason he saw her was because he was spying on her apartment with binoculars (in the film, Doris gets a chance to turn the tables on him).

Not only does the film contain scenes which take place outside Felix's apartment, it also expands the cast to more than two characters. In the play, we occasionally hear the neighbors yelling and knocking on the walls about the racket Doris and Felix are making, but in the screen version some of them actually make an appearance. During a conversation with the landlord (Jacques Sandulescu), Felix learns that someone has been complaining about the noise his typewriter makes. Other than letting it slip that the person is a "she," the landlord doesn't name names. But Felix has his suspicions. When asked by Doris why he ratted on her, Felix throws back the fact that he knows she complained about him, revealing that he knew it was her. We are left wondering if such knowledge perhaps played a part in him wanting revenge.

Felix acts very superior to Doris and, in the play, this results in more of a Pygmalion situation, wherein he tries to force her to learn new words and sets traps for her, all so he can feel better about falling for a woman he never would've pegged as his type. In the screen version, Streisand is utterly charming as Doris, especially when she gets thrown off by Felix's words.

That's not to say Felix isn't lousy in the film. While Doris knows he is engaged before they have sex, Felix is too busy trying to prove his manhood (both the film and the play show '70s homophobia) to care about letting her know about his fiancée, Anne (Barbara Anson). This becomes even more apparent when Felix invites Doris to Anne's parents' house, where he's been staying. Doris doesn't realize that's where they're going, and Felix never acts like it's a

a cynical New Yorker. She's not naïve. She knows if she accepts the ride, there'll probably be strings attached, but she takes the chance anyway and tries not to assume the worst.

In any case, instead of following Doris and the man indoors, there's a sharp cut and Ross' camera turns left to watch another man running up to the same building. This is our introduction to Felix. Segal's body language in this scene is terrific, as he immediately goes to check his mailbox. He's carrying a book (which turns out to be Henry James' 'The Art of the Novel') and instead of tucking it under his arm or putting it down, he puts it in his mouth so he can get out his key. It's already in

his mouth when he walks through the door so it's clear he really wants this mail - and when he opens one of the letters it's apparent why - but it's a rejection letter. We don't know Felix's name yet, but we already know he's a writer, a struggling one at that.

Much in the same way that they meet in the play, Doris and Felix meet after he calls the landlord on her for prostitution. Doris gets kicked out of her apartment and, since it's the middle of the night, decides to knock on Felix's door for help.

There is one difference. In the play, Felix doesn't have another motive for calling the landlord on Doris. Prostitution is illegal. He saw her exchanging money with a man so he big deal. By switching Anne's career from poet to piano player, Henry's screenplay comments on the awkwardness of the situation by having Felix wake up the next morning to the sound of Doris playing.

While Felix might be too frazzled and delusional to realize he's in the wrong, Henry's screenplay isn't. That's another reason why it's so important that the film allows Doris and Felix to leave his apartment. It puts Felix and Doris on equal footing. Doris isn't the only one getting kicked out of apartments. Felix gets kicked out of his too. In order to help Doris get rid of hiccups, Felix puts on a skeleton costume to scare her. Anne Roth's costumes in the film are iconic (particularly Doris' negligee with the handprints across her chest), and the skeleton costume is a far better means of scaring Doris than pretending to strangle her (like he does in the play). In fact, it's so effective that the ensuing commotion raises their landlord.

Felix might think he's better than Doris but he's also just as much of a nuisance when they go to stay with Felix's friend, Barry (Robert Klein). It's never just Doris who is the problem nor Felix who is the innocent victim. Because other people witness their behavior, Felix isn't able to paint himself as a saint.

That being said, Ross does give the final moments of the movie to Felix, who again takes out his insecurities on Doris by taking offense to her saying they "made love." The conversation is very similar to one they have in the play but, in both cases, Felix has no qualms about getting rough with her. He gets away with being abusive, and the film ends with them still together. There's even the implication that Doris has reformed, with her referring to herself as a "former hooker." *The Owl and the Pussycat* mostly calls Felix out on his b.s., but despite that, the ending still does Doris dirty.

TO BE SAVAGE, HUNGRY AND FREE

Allen Rubinstein examines several '70s entries in the 'Wild Child' sub-genre.

"I do not have an original thought. I am screwed; I speak English. That's it. I was not born in a vacuum. Every thought I have belongs to somebody else."
- Lenny Bruce, 1961

Before 1970 there was *2001*.

When Stanley Kubrick's grand masterpiece was released in 1968 to fiercely split reviews ("A monumentally unimaginative movie," said Pauline Kael), Warner Brothers' roadshow release actually came in at a financial loss given the high expense of its production. It wasn't until its re-release in 1971, and an even bigger one in 1974, that *A Space Odyssey* grew into a sensation, retroactively becoming 1968's highest grossing movie. The studio shifted its ad campaign to feature the trippiness of the sci-fi trip once they realized the counterculture had fully embraced the film while passing around funny little cigarettes. For multiple reasons, *2001* is a creature of the '70s.

Those audiences were, in fact, interested in more than just getting on board Kubrick's intense visual ride through space. One viewer in San Francisco ran directly through the (surely expensive) movie screen, shouting: "It's God!" Kubrick's themes were on people's minds. He ushered in the greatest era of American filmmaking with one of the boldest, most audacious, awe-inspiring statements ever put on film, across millions of years and hundreds of millions of miles, unfurling the evolution and transcendence of the human race itself. To do so within a still-unsurpassed technical and visual spectacle - sequences as iconic in today's culture as anything in *The Wizard of Oz* or *Casablanca* - ranks it as one of the great art works of the 20th century. *2001: A Space Odyssey* is revolutionary in every way possible.

It opens with 'The Dawn of Man'.

Those are four very important words. Without that title alerting viewers, the connection of the monkeys on screen to early mankind would be mere vague inference. Played by mimes in elaborate costumes, nothing in their scenes distinguishes them from any ordinary species of Hominin. They are ruthless, without ethical or moral code, aimed purely at self-interest and survival, something not changed, but aided by the arrival of something impossible - right angles, flat surfaces, solid black, an edifice not found

in nature as we know it. The monolith opens them up somehow to discover the new, to invent. The monkeys soon extend their beings with tools (i.e. weapons) for the first time in their existence signaling their step toward the technology which the bulk of the film will explore.

That moment of "something impossible" is precisely what I'm unfolding below. A particular fascination of mine is a narrow sub-genre I call the "unsullied man" drama. They are characters who approach our modern world without context, without ideas about what they'll receive and often without language of any kind. Before this era, it mostly arrived as "noble savage" films, romanticized colonialist ideas personified with the likes of Tarzan or Mowgli. The stories continue to bring us untested protagonists every so often in movies such as *Nell,* Charlie Kaufman's *Human Nature,* the recent Oscar-nominated *Room, Bad Boy Bubby* and *Princess Mononoke.*

What we have here then is a series of case studies. I'm coalescing the findings across the sciences - A feral child raised by a pack of wolves or dogs, an adult raised to maturity in an empty cellar, the pubescent son of a shipwrecked married couple, a primitive mud person magically transformed into a capitalist. They're film characters of the '70s devoid of social rules, absent the programming of church, schools, politics, media and the family unit. They are pure, stripped of modern life with all its benefits and burdens.

It's a life experience so foreign that centering a story on such characters is an exercise of the imagination. How does an evolved brain process new information without names; without language of any kind? What do they gain? What do they lose? Is the journey worthwhile? Do these tormented souls ever reach the vaunted transcendent freedom of *2001's* space baby, floating through outer space, newborn, their eyes wide open to the possibilities.

These characters are untainted by humanity, but they are still human. They still have a past (however limited), biological drives, wants and needs, our species' retinue of emotions and our instinctual base responses to stimuli. The same sun rises and sets on them as the rest of mankind, but the strange sensations they experience when "something impossible" appears is nothing they can articulate in their pre-language state, even to themselves. It's that imaginative leap the storytellers must take that makes the "unsullied man" sub-genre so compelling, and it's only by drawing the subjects of these stories closer to modern civilization that we can start to comprehend their journey and draw our own meaning from it.

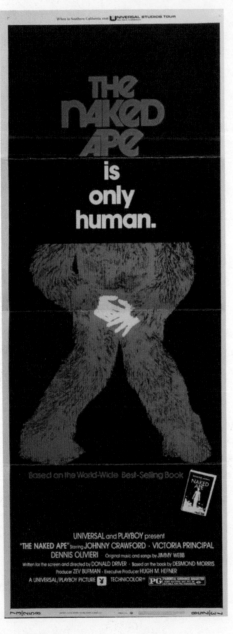

For an era so preoccupied with freedom, it's a revealing tension. The bikers of *Easy Rider,* and so many other disaffected characters in the early '70s, were 'free' because they had a modicum of resources, substances to alter their consciousness, and the open road. They reflected the communes, back-to-the-land organic farm communities and collections of street hippies across the United States (though San Francisco gets all the credit) who chose to live free of rampant consumerism, the day-to-day work grind (known then as 'the rat race'), the nuclear family, and repressive values of the culture at large. Feminists, gay people, native Americans, blacks and the incarcerated all struggled within their movements to be free from bigotry and oppression in all forms from the patriarchy in the halls of power, housing discrimination, police harassment and just general public sentiment. Young men wanted freedom from the draft and the right to vote.

This collective Venn diagram threw down a single gauntlet to mainstream society - 'evolve'. Shed your toxic ideas and become your better selves, the one that recognizes the worth of all people and all ways of being. Let go of the mechanisms of control and scarcity that arrests your development from monkey to space baby. Within that outcry, filmmakers, experiencing their own newfound freedom in the industry's marketplace of ideas, in part asked the question: if we want change, if history has given us this remarkable opportunity to change, what about us can never change? What is immutable? If we rebuilt from the ground up, what would be left?

Part of the answer arrived just one year after *2001* from English zoologist, ethologist and surrealist painter John Desmond Morris with his 1969 non-fiction book 'The Naked Ape: A Zoologist's Study of the Human Animal'. A runaway bestseller, and one of the most influential books of its time, Morris simply applied his methods for studying the life habits of animals to people, framing our behavior as a product of the evolutionary selection process and raw animal instinct. Couplehood and marriage was 'pair bonding' with its rituals determined, not by cultural mores or Dear Abby, but by circumstances that would engineer the greatest likelihood of healthy

ever need on a remote patch of earth containing only he and his parents. There isn't much talking in *The Savage is Loose* past the halfway mark.

You see, David has gone through puberty, and there are no other women on the island save his youthful, attractive mother. The story comes down to a competition between two taboos - incest and filicide (the killing of one's own child). David's only knowledge of the populated world comes from his mother's stories of dances and young

reproduction. The stigma against adultery exists not from the Bible or the patriarchy, but the ability of the male of the species to ensure a clean lineage.

Fortunately for the purposes of this article, they made 'The Naked Ape' into a movie, though in this case "they" means 'Playboy' and "made a movie" means "assembled eighty minutes of footage". *The Naked Ape* movie is one of those shaggy oddities dotting the '70s film landscape. Part film essay, part reenactment in short skits, part animated vignettes, it's structured more like an instructional movie for classrooms than a proper film, shoveling quotes from the book at us in bulk.

It's not hard to imagine why Hugh Hefner would be interested in this material, though the film he funded couldn't be tamer. For one, it's made clear that of the primates, man has the largest penis, but the book and film also explore what underlies our cultural need for sexual repression. Males having evolved through natural selection to be the 'sexual hunter', the advent of advanced civilization in only a few thousand years necessitates that we learn how to not act out every urge. The speed of a developing society easily overtook the eons-slow pace of natural selection, and those who met the new demands with fear and self-loathing need to project their urges onto others as 'sin'.

What passes for a protagonist in *The Naked Ape* - former child western star Johnny Crawford just trying to find the meaning of it all, man - listens to his English Lit. professor talk about erotic fiction. "During every uptight era, the man with the pen seems not only to let himself be free enough to investigate the myriad pleasures afforded by love, but it is because one poet's vivid and inventive imagination must serve for the many. He is given license, become the symbol of the free spirit, the fulfilled man, a luxury not afforded the masses." Apart from the wonderfully dated references and slang, *The Naked Ape* is one of the only films under consideration here that directly addresses human sexuality, and does so in an appropriately upfront and candid way.

Then there's the other one - a story venturing into far riskier territory. *The Savage is Loose* is a 1974 film directed by George C. Scott, starring Scott and his wife Trish Van Devere as a married couple, John and Maida, who in 1902 are stranded by shipwreck on a deserted island with their infant son, David. Their hopes of rescue fading as the years pass, they turn their attention to raising David with the skills and grit to survive in the pitiless environment of the wilderness that has claimed them. He will be of the island, subject to the laws of nature not man, although he is unique among these characters in that he has all the language he will

No woman is an island ...forever.

21

romance, something Scott's character warns her against. David has no outlet, only empty, tormented fantasies of the joy of 'pair bonding' and the Bible stories they've also raised him on - a head full of contradictions and warring impulses.

The first inklings of David's pursuit of his mother are, well, creepy. It's clear that he functions on a different presence in the world than his parents, ominous and primal and ready for the hunt. John is driven to where he feels he has no other option but to bring a machete onto the boy they raised, but before that happens, David breaks down, revealing the torment, confusion and despair he's experiencing. John is about to fatally break the stalemate, when Maida reaches her own critical decision. Here's the spoiler - incest wins. This is her son, and they are alone. The credits roll before any potential consequences emerge from her choice, but what can it matter to give him this with no other options and nobody to ever judge or interfere? Their circumstances are unique.

I won't plant a flag that *The Savage is Loose* is any kind of undiscovered gem of the decade, but it is certainly compelling. David never has to navigate the complexities of the real world, so his dilemmas are quite basic. It's his parents who have to do the heavy lifting of breaking away from societal rules. Setting the story just after the turn of the 20th century only impacts the story in John and Maida's dedication to living according to the Bible, a book with all kinds of things to say about incestuous relationships. The story David focuses on is an unspoken one he has to figure out himself - the impossibility of Cain and Abel's wives, how they must have been daughters of Adam and Eve and thus their sisters.

He is clearly missing nothing in terms of intelligence, resourcefulness or his thirst to live, yet his lack of context in the world, his lack of grounding in mores or socialization makes his internal conflicts and unmet instinctual needs a mortal threat, not only to the two people he loves the most, but the only individuals he has ever known or likely ever will. That they acquiesce to his desires is actually *their* evolution into *his* world, shedding the taboos of civilization they've left behind to live as beasts in nature.

In yet another refraction of this dynamic, an unusual

project from 1977 fits into the "unsullied man" genre, a TV-movie about a character that shares many traits with David. The TV movie *Lucan* was a pilot of a series about the journey of a feral child who was found and educated well before the story begins. Now 25 years old, Lucan is leaving the scientific institute where he's lived, ready to make his way in the world and find his natural parents. Kevin Murphy in his first role plays the title character, the actor having vaguely animal-like features and long, flowing locks of hair. The premise rests on the conceit that, having been raised by wolves, Lucan has a special bond with nature and animals that gives him great strength and agility, heightened senses and a quasi-psychic connection that makes his eyes glow yellow for some reason. He interprets conflict using animal logic and spouts dialogue that could have been lifted directly from *The Naked Ape*.

This being a TV effort of the late '70s, there's a level of

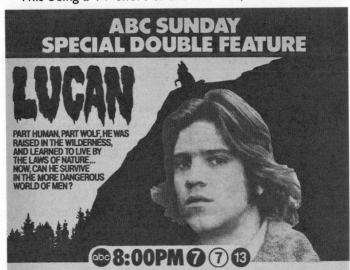

silliness involved, but the idea is intriguing that with his now-developed understanding of modern life, he could be a powerful person in the world by bringing his animal-self to any set of circumstances. This is not a fish-out-of-water story. It's stated that he has the heart rate and blood pressure of the creatures who brought him up, meaning that his physical body patterned itself after his non-human adopted parents. The series itself lasted all of twelve episodes and apparently didn't live up to the pilot's promising start, but this is still a unique entry that hews a bit more closely to the era's back-to-the-land ideas, fantastic or otherwise, that building a connection to the natural world is a natural bulwark against those city-folk caught up in their day-to-day illusions and technical knowhow.

Another television piece worth mentioning is *Stalk the Wild Child* (1976), a smarter but more stock account of a fictional modern-day feral child they call Cal, taken in by a scientist and his assistant who become surrogate parents, and eventually a married couple. The first half covers the rescue and recovery journey beat for beat as it's told in

Truffaut's *The Wild Child* which I'll get to below. The second half of the film jumps forward toward looking at the cost of Cal's notoriety as the scientists' study, conducted by Cal's parental figures played by stodgy David Janssen and, once again, Trish Van Devere, is released to the press. The early footage of Cal's animal behavior elicits laughter from reporters, shaming him and driving him to sign a contract with an opportunistic book publisher well-cast with the charisma of Allan Arbus. Cal tries writing his memoirs, falls for the assistant meant to keep him on track and then has artistic differences with Arbus after he crassly commercializes his story. Both this and *Lucan* pose the intriguing question of 'what next' for their young wild men once they have at least enough grounding to function in society, though neither carry the depth to take the full opportunity of this captivating 'what if'.

Which is why it is so satisfying watching two masterful filmmakers - Francois Truffaut and Werner Herzog - take full advantage of this genre in different ways. Comparing these next two films is a riveting exercise.

Truffaut's *The Wild Child* (1970) is foundational text, both in fiction and real life. A true story of the care of a feral child captured from the woods in France in 1788, Truffaut himself plays physician Jean Itard, who disputes the conclusion that the boy is an animalistic brute, possibly deaf mute, who must be institutionalized. Itard was something of an outside-the-box thinker, conducting experiments on deaf children to restore their

hearing with methods like shock treatments and leech therapy. He brings the boy he calls 'Victor' into his home to educate him, aided by his housekeeper, Madame Guerin, with full time funding from the French government. Itard gathered all available literature on child rearing and the behavioral sciences, as well as studying Enlightenment thinkers like Rousseau, Locke and Descartes. The process represented in the film, and Itard's subsequent writings, formed the basis for current methods of helping developmentally stunted individuals. *The Wild Child* shows Itard improvising and experimenting with many of these techniques in real time.

Clearly important things are happening, and Truffaut plays Itard with genuine gravity and purpose. The paces he runs Victor through are strenuous for him, but never cruel or abusive. Itard uses punishment and reward to guide Victor - the punishment little more than a "time out" in the closet for a minute or two - and there's a clear sense he's training the child as one would a dog. This is still the 18th century, where the inner life of children wasn't of much concern in their upbringing. While he receives all the attention any young boy could want, is Victor a human child or a science experiment?

Such is the ambiguity of this deceptively simple three-person docu-drama (largely taken directly from Itard's writings). Madame Guerin gives Victor love and affection, even referring to him as "my boy" by the end of the film. Itard, considerably less so. Absolutely no allowance is given to the emotional trauma Victor is certainly carrying around from being abandoned in the woods at four or five years old (and possibly cut across the neck), having to fend for himself until he was twelve, then being hunted down and sent into a modern civilization he can't begin to fathom. Victor has no frame of reference. He tries to comply with

Itard's lessons to be rewarded, but he doesn't even know what they're for.

Toward the film's end, Victor runs

away when he's denied his customary play time in the outdoors (in reality he fled his conditions nearly a dozen times), and the crux of *The Wild Child* comes fully into focus. Victor tries to mount himself up a tree and fails. He attempts to steal a farmer's chicken and is chased away with pitchforks. His clothing is tattered and filthy, where nine months earlier he lived naked to the elements. Finally, he returns to Itard's home, but his expression looks anything but happy to be back.

Itard and Guerin welcome him: "I'm glad you're home. Do you understand? This is your home. You're no longer a wild boy, even if you're not yet a man." As Victor and Guerin climb the stairs, Itard emits the last line: "Later we'll resume our lessons," and the camera irises in on Victor's impassive, resigned face. He is trapped in the modern living he's become accustomed to, shorn of his free existence in the woods. The price of shoes and milk for Victor is to be subject to this distant man's peculiar exercises and the rules of when he may and may not enjoy his beloved open space. It's heartbreaking.

This is not to imply it would be appropriate to leave feral children to their rough, lonely fate, to die young without boundaries, proper food or human contact, but the larger point would definitely resonate with audiences of the late '60s and early '70s. Be part of society and have safety and community approval, but be owned. Or be hungry, dirty, lawless and free. Neither option is particularly enviable.

Mid-way through the film, Itard makes a stunning admission in a moment of frustration with Victor's lack of progress.

"I give up. I'm wasting my time with you. Sometimes I'm sorry that I know you. I'm discouraged, Victor… and disappointed." Then in narration: "I had barely spoken when I saw his chest heaving noisily and a stream of tears falling from underneath the blindfold. Now, ready to renounce the task I had imposed upon myself, seeing the time I'd wasted and how deeply I regretted having known him, I condemned the curiosity of the men who had wrenched him away from his innocent and happy life."

Itard can't grasp that Victor, while not knowing the words, certainly hears the disapproval. He wants to please Itard, even while he understands very little. What he really needs is parents. Itard never returns to the harshness of that passage, continuing his firm but fair methods. *The Wild Child* never condemns this man of science, and in the end, the question is less interpersonal than existential. It is about the position of the individual being civilized and the civilizers imposing the will of society on an innocent. As with most '70s movies there is no happy ending. Just a light that shines on the tense and unwieldy reality of the human condition.

A whole new set of questions confront us in Werner Herzog's *The Enigma of Kaspar Hauser* (1974), in many ways the corollary to Truffaut's film. Also based on real-life events, Kaspar Hauser's tale is well known in Europe, where the actual truth of the matter is mysterious and heatedly debated. Some think him a fraud and faker, others part of a royal conspiracy, but Herzog tells the story straight, depicting the title character as something of a naïf poet, philosopher and martyr. Kaspar is a stocky older teenager who appears suddenly in a German town in 1828, unable to speak, barely able to walk, a pure blank slate if ever there was one. After much discussion of the peculiar stranger, he is taken in by the townsfolk who try to care for him as a community.

Kaspar Hauser has no wilderness survival skills to escape to. He grew to maturity inside a darkened cell, and is abandoned with a note about his widower father caring for eleven children. Contrary to Victor, Lucan and David, Kaspar is a passive character who does not fight. He even welcomes the townsfolk's attempts to help him learn motor skills, uses a spoon and enjoys food that isn't hunks of bread. He wants to function like an ordinary person, and is often overwhelmed and perplexed by how much he doesn't understand and the shock of being amongst people after a lifetime of complete isolation.

As much as Herzog is taking the historical record at face value, he is sneaking in his own satirical edge by recurrently putting Kaspar in a room with local clergy, town

L'ENFANT SAUVAGE de François TRUFFAUT

bureaucrats, intellectuals and stuffy noblemen, letting this man-child puncture their various pretensions with innocent observations. At one point, he asks one of the matrons what the purpose of women might be, since all they seem to do is knit and cook food (the matron tells him to go ask a man). This is Herzog using the genre more toward its original intention, to see our lives from an outside perspective, to expose our vices and silly ideas through new eyes.

As Hauser increases his vocabulary, he tries to write his biography and takes up piano. Hearing music for the first time brings Kaspar to a flood of tears, saying: "It fills my heart." The natural world and art deeply affects him, as all of it is brand new. He also begins envisioning stories - poetic allegories for life and death, which are also show up in his dreams (he never dreamed in the cell). Again, the use of an "unsullied man" presents us with a vision of our fundamental conditions on earth, focusing in on what's important while eliding our jadedness and conditioning.

Finally, there's *Savages*, a surreal 1972 Merchant-Ivory production, virtually unfindable and magnificent. The movie opens in sepia tone with the mud people examined by the camera with ethnographic intertitles and untranslated male and female German narration. The mud people are a primitive tribe wearing ritual masks, nearly naked, grabbing what they desire from one another's hands and humping each other at random moments.

They are about to sacrifice the priestess' consort when something impossible intrudes; the perfect sphere of a croquet ball comes sailing through their environment. They follow its path, and come upon an old estate, abandoned, coated in cobwebs, still full of belonging that they begin haphazardly rummaging through. They encounter and grope at stairs, windows, clothes. Twenty-five minutes into the film the screen cuts to color, where the cast becomes modern Englishers. They look refined but act like selfish children with only the outward trappings of civilization. However, by the time dinner arrives - immediately after the cast encounters the corpse of a borzoi pure-bred dog - they are full-blown aristocrats, capitalists, sophisticates, playboys and socialites. The portrait is a send up of F. Scott Fitzgerald character types and a reversal of Luis Bunuel's *The Exterminating Angels* - a dinner party where bestial people become civilized instead of the other way around. One male actor plays a female character and vice versa so it's clear that these are meant to be avatars, not human beings. The character names themselves say as much. Sam Waterston plays James - The Limping Man; Warhol Factory member Ultra Violet is Lliona - A Decadent.

The ensemble has no awareness of the change that's taken place, even as the conversation turns directly to the remote mud people of Africa and the annual ritual sacrifice of the priestess' consort. They call the mud people the "most interesting people on the continent," until Sir Harry, the older member, mentions the recent annihilation of the tribe. Dinner continues. The guests gossip, spread rumors, play power games. They fornicate in corners and lie to

individuals determining their place in groups and systems they grew up well outside of. Truffaut told a reporter about *The Wild Child*: "I did not want to spell out my message. It is simply this: man is nothing without other men." The privileged men and women of *Savages* are the other men, and the verdict is not good.

Nonetheless, these stories depict the variety of ways other men choose to absorb one who is not one of theirs, not steeped in their assumptions and shared illusions. If those lost children work hard enough, they could be part of collective action that is savage and brutal, but also full

one another. Over and over, they discuss the impending collapse of different cultures, economies, governments, all deeply convincing and all complete fiction. The psychodrama is taking place only within those walls.

Gradually, the conversation becomes more obtuse, the activity more fragmented, the references more surreal. They become crueler to each other as they begin regressing back to their savage state. Waterston, who played the consort about to die, catapults into the pool to drown three times in quick succession. Another female hangs herself. Soon they are scrabbling with one another in a pile of coal for shiny objects. Finally, they are on the lawn, in a frenzy of croquet balls and mallets before following the magical orbs back into the woods.

Savages is not a subtle critique. It doesn't ask: "What does civilization offer and what does it take away?" Instead, it comes down firmly to tell the audience that civilization is nothing but performance, our intellects rationalizing our animal instincts. It's a deeply cynical film, circling right back to the beginning of *2001*, with gangs of monkeys beating each other over their share of wild boar.

The young men in these films (and they're all men) are

Starring Susie Blakely Margaret Brewster Thayer David Neil Fitzgerald Anne Francine Salome Jens Martin Kove Christopher Pennock Asha Puthli Eva Saleh Paulita Sedgewick Louis Stadlen Bryss Thacker Ultra Violet Sam Waterston Kathleen Widdoes Director James Ivory Producer Ismail Merchant Screenplay by George Swift Trow and Michael O'Donoghue Music Joe Raposo Photography Walter Lassally B.S.C. Associate Producer Anthony Korner Executive Producer Joseph J.M.Saleh Produced In Association With Merchant Ivory Productions Released By Angelika Films

of energy for something greater.

The children of the WWII generation, living through the Vietnam War, injected their perspective into the American film industry during a rare historical occurrence. The necessity for humanity to evolve, to step up to itself, was front and center in their thinking. Can we become the space baby? That floating infant is haunting because it is ambiguous and pointedly non-specific as a single sublime image closing out a two-hour-twenty-minute soul journey. Kubrick wouldn't be foolish enough to portray what human enlightenment might look like, so it remains a symbol, an idea, an uncertain placeholder representing that elusive something we might someday be.

STAR TREK
THE MOTION PICTURE ™
Boldly going where the TV show had gone before

by Martin Dallard

It wasn't supposed to be a major motion picture at all; rather a new and on-going television series called *Star Trek: Phase II*. But in La La Land, things often don't turn out the way they're planned. More about that later...

Let us start with the story. Several years have passed since the *USS Enterprise* and her intrepid crew returned to Earth from their 5-year mission into the vastness of space, the final frontier. Since then, Captain James T. Kirk (William Shatner) has been promoted to Admiral, while Science Officer Spock has returned to his home world Vulcan to purge himself of his half-human emotions and become a being of pure logic through the mystical Vulcan ritual of Kolinar. Many of the crew have gone their own way too. Others, like Chief Engineer Montgomery Scott (James Doohan), have remained to work on a major refit of the *Enterprise*, getting her ready for her next stint of deep space exploration.

In the meantime, a mysterious gigantic blue space cloud has been detected heading Earth's way, destructively wiping out all life along its route. The only Federation starship close enough to intercept the cloud (and maybe figure out what it's seeking) is the *Enterprise*, though she's barely ready for such an important mission, still being docked in space following her refit.

Due to his experience and knowledge, Kirk is reappointed as the commander of the *Enterprise*. The barely space-worthy ship and its mainly fledgling crew are assigned to set out to try and stop the cloud before it reaches Earth's orbit. Along the way, Kirk finds himself dealing with more than just the hostile cloud. He has problems with some of the crew too, in particular Captain Decker (Stephen Collins) who was about to be sworn in as Kirk's successor at the helm of the *Enterprise*. He's rightly angry about playing second fiddle to anyone, especially since he was so

close to assuming captaincy of the ship. It doesn't help that Kirk hasn't logged any space time for several years, while Decker has personally overseen the refit of the *Enterprise* and knows the upgraded systems better than anyone.

Can Kirk win a fight on both fronts, or is it too much for even a legend like him to handle?

It was in December, 1979, when *Star Trek: The Motion Picture* hit the big screen, It should have been an immediate home run, especially since fans of the TV franchise had waited years for something like this to come to fruition. A feature length spin-off of their favourite show must have seemed like a dream come true. But upon release, the film got mixed reviews from critics and the cinema-going public alike. Against a budget of $46,000,000 - a staggering amount for the time - it reaped $140,000,000 at the global box office, a hefty chunk of change even back then but still significantly short of Paramount's expectations.

Both *Star Wars* and *Close Encounters of the Third Kind* had been released prior to *Trek,* and both had achieved critical acclaim and massive financial success, reinvigorating the public's hunger for sci-fi and fantasy films. Surely, Paramount figured, *Star Trek* - being the granddaddy of

them all - should have cleaned up at the box office. After all, it was the original space-going show on TV and already had an enormous built-in fan base. It was only logical to expect these fans to flock to the cinema in droves, again and again.

What caused the lower-than-expected box office performance? A bad script? Possibly poor direction? Was there too much studio interference, which had been known to happen on huge projects like this? Maybe all of the above? We need to travel back in time (something that *Trek* had handled on several occasions) to get to the root of the problem.

After the original show was cancelled in 1969, its creator Gene Roddenberry thought there were still more tales to tell and continually lobbied Paramount about producing a film depicting the further adventures of Kirk and crew. Although the show was no more, it was still regularly shown in worldwide syndication and was becoming more popular than ever, proving there was still life in the old space dog yet.

Paramount could see the logic (no pun intended,) in what Roddenberry was pushing for. Although many

writers stepped up with scenarios and potential story outlines, the studio honchos weren't happy with what they were reading. They felt maybe the best way forward was to return the franchise to its grass roots, where there had been success in the past. So, by the mid '70s, they gave the go-ahead for a new TV show set in the *Trek* universe. This would have been the aforementioned *Star Trek: Phase II*.

In 1977, test filming got underway to bring *Trek* back to the small screen. But that same year, both *Star Wars* and *Close Encounters* struck box office gold, inspiring Paramount to take a swing at a big screen *Star Trek* entry.

Finally settling on Academy Award-winning director Robert Wise, who'd previous dabbled in the sci-fi genre

with *The Day the Earth Stood Still*, the film was greenlit with a budget of under $20,000,000. A director of Wise's stature brought a lot of gravitas to the production, and at last it seemed as if the project was being treated seriously.

The original crew of the *Enterprise* were signed on to return, though Leonard Nimoy dragged his feet initially due to some financial wrangling. Eventually, though, a deal was struck and the whole band was back together once more. There was a little more to-ing and fro-ing over the script, with both Shatner and Nimoy given final approval… but at last - at long bloody last - *Star Trek* was off to the races!

There were a few extra faces added to make up the crew, two particularly key ones being Collins as Captain Decker and Persis Khambatta as his lost love interest Ilia. In fact, these two new characters become integral to the plot and play a significant part in the big climax.

Special effects duties fell to the legendary Douglas Trumbull, who was ably assisted by John Dykstra and Richard Yuricich (both heavy hitters in the field). They needed to be on top of their game to match or surpass the effects that cinemagoers were now used to thanks to the likes of *Star Wars*. Initially, Trumbull passed on the project as he wanted to focus on his directing skills, so Paramount had to look elsewhere.

It fell to Robert Abel and his effects company to do the heavy lifting, but it soon became apparent that they were punching above their weight. Their designs were well conceived, but they lacked the experience to handle a film of this size. It wasn't long before Paramount was in trouble and running way behind schedule.

Abel and his crew left the production after a year of hard work with not a lot of film in the can. Trumbull had been helping Abel as an executive while trying to get a film of his own off the ground. But

his project fell through, and Trumbull became available full time. Paramount gave him carte blanche, as long as he could get all the optical effects done within the time frame. He knew it *could* be done, but it meant the effects budget virtually doubled as the race to meet the ambitious release date of December 1979 loomed ever closer.

This is where John Dykstra came on board, having just

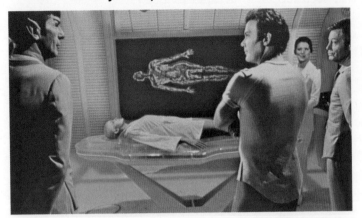

started up his own company after leaving Industrial Light and Magic. Wise was very keen to emphasise that the *USS Enterprise*, a very real and essential member of the cast, needed to look better than she had during her days of whizzing across the small screen in everyone's living room. And so the grand old space duchess had a complete overhaul, which can be seen in all its glory in the scene in the space dock, where Scotty accompanies Kirk as he does a fly-by of the new and improved vessel before boarding her for the first time in years. Their shuttle traverses the outer hull of the ship, giving them (and us) a gloriously detailed look at the new *Enterprise*. It's not just Kirk whose mouth drools at the sight of his old mistress - we're right there drooling with him!

It has been said that the camera lingers a little too long during this scene, but the *Enterprise* deserves her moment in the spotlight. No-one had ever seen her look so grand on screen before, and it's obvious that this is the lady who holds the key to Kirk's heart. No wonder he fought Starfleet to get back his command. And if we're honest, this is the closest thing to space porn we'll ever get!

Composer Jerry Goldsmith was approached to do the score, and he exceeded all expectations. His new *Star Trek* theme became so iconic that it was used for the rebooted '80s television show *Star Trek: The Next Generation*. Goldsmith had been Roddenberry's top choice to compose the score for the original TV show, but scheduling problems knocked that idea on the head. So, when the big screen version was greenlit, Roddenberry was eager to recommend Goldsmith to director Wise. Wise couldn't have agreed more, having already worked with the composer on a previous production. They were already good friends, and Goldsmith willingly came aboard. So good was the relationship between him and Paramount that Goldsmith returned to the franchise several times to compose for future *Trek* entries, chief among them *Star Trek: Nemesis*.

For the first outing, electronic synthesisers were used to great effect, especially during the trippy space cloud sequences when the Klingons, the *Enterprise*, and finally Spock pierce its voluminous veil and reach the machine planet nestled, hidden, at its heart. The whole sequence has a '70s disco vibe, with the machine world and its surrounding structures being cold and barren, devoid of feeling, warmth and emotion. Goldsmith's keyboard captures this perfectly, giving everything a clinical, almost sterile ambience. And to the delight of fans of the TV show, Goldsmith manages to weave into his musical narrative the original TV theme composed by Alexander Courage. It's a nice nod to the franchise's roots. I have to admit that upon hearing it for the first time during the cinematic release, it brought a tear to my teenage eye. (Naturally, I didn't admit this to my girlfriend at the time... I think I told her I'd poked myself in the eye with a Kia-Ora straw!)

original show was slower paced at times, more cerebral, not so outright gung-ho. To use a musical analogy to describe them, *Star Wars* would be a Rolling Stones concert while *Star Trek the Motion Picture* would be a grand opera. And that's the difference at their core.

I've always been more than happy to get the best of both worlds, but I think if *Star Trek* had debuted before *Star Wars* on the big screen, it might have been met with more welcoming arms. The phenomenal success of George Lucas' indie spacefaring project left audiences wanting more. If the editing on *Star Trek* had been a little tighter, with fewer of those lingering shots of jaw dropping space scenes where very little actually happens, then perhaps this may have helped too. More scenes with the old triumvirate of Kirk, Spock and Bones wouldn't have gone amiss either.

But the whole production had been an uphill struggle from the very start. With effects problems being one of the main things to hinder the making of the film, it's amazing it was finished at all. In fact, legend has it that director Wise got the final cut in the can a mere two days before the film's big premiere in Washington! He reportedly delivered it personally to the theatre for its first showing!

But doesn't that seem somehow ironic? Whatever scrape Kirk and crew found themselves in, they always seemed to get away with it by the skin of their teeth at the eleventh hour. Wise and crew certainly found themselves in the same boat, and there's a certain symbiosis to that which, maybe, is how it should be.

Star Trek: The Motion Picture is by no means perfect. In fact, I don't think a "perfect movie" actually exists, as there will always be a detractor or two out there no matter what the film. But it does deserve a second chance from those who weren't enamoured with it first time around. In more recent years, there has been a Director's Cut released to DVD and Blu Ray, which many feel is an improvement over the original theatrical cut.

I could wax lyrical about this film until we reach the 23rd century, but I'm more inclined to encourage viewers to discover (or rediscover) its delights for themselves. Do yourself a favour: beam yourself down to the surface, set Phasers to stun and prepare to explore the undiscovered country. A word to the wise, though: always check the colour of your shirt!

The dastardly Klingons get their own theme too, harsh and imperialistic in tone, almost militaristic, excellently capturing the id of the barbarian race it represents. They couldn't have asked for a better composer - Goldsmith's score is the beating heart of the film.

The main problem with the picture seems to be the pacing, and indeed, this was something that was addressed in its sequel (*Star Trek: The Wrath of Khan*) which is a different animal altogether. We'd all seen the television show, and were used to seeing Kirk get into fights, with his shirt inevitably being torn asunder. There would often be the death of a crewman aboard the *Enterprise*, typically one who was wearing a red shirt. They always seemed like lemmings, only too eager to leap off that perilous cliff for the cause! And naturally, Kirk would get the girl, or alien as was sometimes the case.

Admittedly, the first film is a tad ponderous (*Star Trek: The Motionless Picture* being one of the crueller nicknames given to it), but in its defence I think Roddenberry wanted to get back to this sort of 'thinking man's' sci-fi. The

A Deep Dive into Deep End

by David Michael Brown

Opening with a splash of red blood that will haunt proceedings until the shocking denouement and Cat Stevens singing *But I Might Die Tonight, Deep End* views the '60s - that most swinging of decades - through the dark fractured lens of the '70s. The once freewheeling, liberated era that had seen the British capital become a Mecca for sex, drugs and rock 'n' roll is here portrayed as the locale for a dour kitchen sink drama, albeit a delightfully quirky one full of oddball characters and an infectious Krautrock soundtrack.

For a film that so astutely portrays the excitement of youth and the potential of the times, it also delights in letting down its protagonists. This is a cautionary coming-of-age tale of drab disillusionment. As directed by Polish auteur Jerzy Skolimowski, his askew view of London (the bulk of the film was shot in Munich) is delightfully esoteric. The iconoclastic filmmaker, boxer, poet and painter began his career in his homeland in the early '60s as a screenwriter for Andrzej Wajda (*Innocent Sorcerers*) and Roman Polanski (*Knife in the Water*), before directing a series of radical, highly personal films like *Walkover* (1965), *Identification Marks: None* (1965) and *Barrier* (1966). In the '70s and '80s, he went on to work as an ex-pat in Europe and America on films like *The Shout* (1978) with Alan Bates and *Moonlighting* (1982) starring Jeremy Irons, both of which won at the Cannes Film Festival. And in 1970, the prolific talent made a splash with *Deep End*.

Originally named *Starting Out*, the film follows naïve 15-year-old, Mike (newcomer John Moulder-Brown), who starts work as a bathhouse attendant at a delightfully dilapidated swimming pool. He quickly develops a crush on his older, attractive, aloof and ever-so-groovy co-worker Susan (Jane Asher). They become tentative friends, sharing tricks to get bigger tips by looking after the opposite sex. In the heady mix of chlorine, shampoo and scrubbed floors, the inexperienced young lad soon becomes infatuated with his glamorous workmate. The feeling isn't mutual though, and Susan plays with his affections. Mike feels shunned, especially when he discovers that Susan has a fiancé who she is cheating on with an older, married man (Karl Michael Vogler) Worse, the older guy was formerly Mike's physical education teacher and also works at the baths as a swimming instructor for teenage girls. Mike begins stalking Susan when she leaves the confines of the pool, and his innocent crush quickly spirals into obsession.

The angry adolescent follows Susan and her playboy boyfriend Chris (Christopher Sandford) to a cinema, actually the now-closed Regal Cinema on Hale End Road in East London. The fleapit is screening *Dr. Lotte Fiedler's The Science of Sex*. Mike takes a seat behind the couple and makes a nuisance of himself while the monochrome sex film - complete with titillating glimpses of nudity, a sanctimonious Teutonic narration and bombastic 'Ride of the Valkyries' soundtrack - entertains the giggling raincoat brigade. He kisses Susan's arm before caressing her from behind. Soon Chris calls the management who, in turn, call the police. The speed at which our wide-eyed, inexperienced 'hero' ditches his schoolboy innocence for toxic masculinity is alarming. It makes Mike even more fascinating to watch but less likable as the film's main protagonist.

And then there's the night Mike spends in Soho as he

pursues Susan and her playboy fiancé into a 'member's only' nightclub called Skull. Baulking at the entry price, he loiters outside buying hot dogs from a local street vendor, played by Burt Kwouk (best known as Kato in the *Pink Panther* films). The pair build a nice comic relationship as Mike awkwardly bows every time he orders another "with mustard?" As the Soho nightlife bustles around the teenager, he steals a life-sized standee of a scantily clad model who looks suspiciously like Susan from outside a strip show ("It's Angelica Continental, from Manchester.") He escapes the wrath of the irate geezer standing in front of the dodgy establishment by hiding in the room of a bored prostitute with a broken leg. On an overcrowded street corner - Walker's Court on Brewer Street - Skolimowski manages to epitomise a Soho of a bygone era, the seedier side of the glamorous chic so stylishly portrayed in Edgar Wright's *Last Night in Soho* (2021). The whole sequence is soundtracked by *Mother Sky*, a grinding 14 minutes of fuzzed-up psychedelia by German rockers Can, the pioneers of kosmische musik. Written by the band's exalted members Holger Czukay, Jaki Liebezeit, Michael Karoli, Irmin Schmidt and then-new singer Damo Suzuki specifically for the film, the track featured on the band's album *Soundtracks* released in 1970.

The night ends in the London Underground as Mike, complete with standee, confronts Susan to find out if the model is her while aghast commuters watch the unfolding melee. It's one of the few scenes where Munich wasn't masquerading as the Big Smoke. Other British locations included various London streets where Mike cycles and Cathall Road Baths and Fulham Pool where the interior scenes of the pool were shot. The labyrinthian corridors and changing rooms were shot at the Müllersches Volksbad on Rosenheimer Straße 1 in Munich. It's indicative of the brilliance of Charly Steinberger's work on the film that at no time do you think you are watching a film shot in Germany, even though local actors were used and dubbed into English. When Mike crashes into a police box, it was the very same prop used as Peter Cushing's TARDIS in his two mid-'60s films *Dr. Who and the Daleks* (1965) and *Daleks' Invasion Earth 2150 A.D.* (1966).

The film is striking for many reasons, but there is no denying the importance of the casting of the two leads. Asher is sensational as the self-destructive Susan, clad in the epitome of '60s fashion including white boots and a fabulous yellow plastic raincoat. She is a flirt and a tease who, despite being engaged, has illicit affairs with her customers, much to the chagrin of her young

workmate. Within the peeling walls of the bathhouse, she is Mike's friend. But outside, in the cold streets of wintry London, she antagonises and taunts him, playing with his obvious affections. "Jerzy told me it was seeing me in a TV play in a series called *Wicked Women*, where I played a real-life Victorian murderess called Anne Marie Moody, that led him to cast me as Susan," she explained.

"I was trying to be very sophisticated, smoking cigarettes

and being cool," John Moulder-Brown told 'The Guardian' when discussing the role of Mike. "I must have looked ridiculous. Jerzy thought I wasn't vulnerable enough, but the producer Judd Bernard persuaded him to give me a screen test, and that convinced him. I was going through the same adolescent period as Mike. Unlike him, I was lucky enough to have had girlfriends, but I still had that rawness. For me, it became all about allowing emotions I understood as a teenager to have a life within the context of the scenes."

Throughout his career, Skolimowski pushed his actors, constantly urging them to dive into their characters and improvise when necessary. While the actors were expected to know the script, they were never expected to stick to the written word. Moulder-Brown remarked: "There's a bit where I'm on my bicycle, riding alongside Jane's car. I was supposed to stop the bike in front of the vehicle, but it was raining, and the brakes didn't work, so the bike skidded, hit the pavement and I went flying. As I was in the air, I remember thinking: 'We've got to keep going because this is going to look great.' When I landed, I could just hear Jerzy calling out: 'Kip feelming! Kip feelming!'"

Skolimowski also cast aging starlet Diana Dors for a memorable scene as Mike's first female customer with an obsession with George Best. The vivacious blonde had made a name for herself in a succession of increasingly saucy ribald comedies and risky sexploitationers like *Yield to the Night* (1956), *The Unholy Wife* (1957) and *Passport to Shame* (1958), along with a turn in William Castle's *Berserk!* (1967) with Joan Crawford. "Diana Dors was a sex symbol during my youth so, when making *Deep End*, I jumped at the opportunity to employ her," Skolimowski told 'Cineaste'. "She seemed surprised to be offered the role. When I asked her to put on the costume I had envisioned for her - a tight, polka-dotted dress - she said: 'So that's how you see me? Well then.' I was very happy with her performance in the film."

In an interview with 'NME' in 1982, David Lynch, the eccentric visual stylist behind *Blue Velvet* (1986), *Wild at Heart* (1990) and *Twin Peaks*, said of Skolimowski's masterpiece: "I don't like colour movies and I can hardly think about colour. It really cheapens things for me and there's never been a colour movie I've freaked out over except one - this thing called *Deep End*, which had really great art direction." The baths are an art deco delight. The corridors are painted a vibrant green with yellow and blue trimmings with stained glassed windows of yellow and orange, matching Asher's vibrant red hair. The aforementioned bloody foreboding is repeated throughout the film. Mike cuts his hand on a shattered piece of glass when he activates the fire alarm to stop Susan and his ex-teacher. While Susan is taunting the baths cashier, played by Erica Beer, a lone painter slaps bright red paint on the

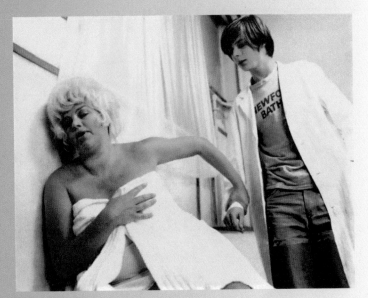

wall behind them in a surreal signpost to the tragedy to come.

And the inevitability of that finale makes it all the more distressing, largely thanks to Asher's perfectly nuanced performance. After Mike tries to disrupt a cross-country run organised by his former sports coach, he gets into a physical fight with Susan. During the fracas, the diamond in her engagement ring is dislodged and falls into the snow. His panicked hackneyed plan is to collect all the snow where the diamond fell in plastic bags and melt it in the swimming pool drained for maintenance. Using a lowered

ceiling lamp outlet to heat an electric kettle in the empty pool, the haphazard idea actually works, but a phone call and an irate lover thwart a proud Mike's plans to take their relationship to the next level. As water pours back into the pool, the couple fight after Susan threatens to leave. Mike swings the lowered lamp in anger and it hits the back of her head and knocks over tins of red paint. She slowly sinks unconscious into the ever-deepening water. The shocked look on her face is heartbreaking as we slowly witness her realisation that she is dying. Her blood mixes with red paint as Mike begins to float with her lifeless body - paralleling the scene when he did the same with the standee he had thrown into the pool - and Cat Stevens' deathly refrain returns, bringing the film full circle.

Little seen on its original release, *Deep End* found itself relegated to the bottom half of a doomed-love double-bill with Franco Zeffirelli's *Romeo and Juliet* (1968) starring Leonard Whiting and Olivia Hussey. It wasn't until it was re-released on the British Film Institute's Flipside label after a brief cinema run in 2011, that it began to receive the accolades it deserved. Ryan Gilbey wrote in 'The Guardian': "What could have been just another coming-of-age story is transformed by an absurdist sensibility, uninhibited performances and a heightened use of colour... a defining British work, as well as one of the most acute screen portraits of London."

It's a testament to the filmmakers that *Deep End*, rather than becoming a vintage curiosity, has stood the test of time. The morally ambiguous script, written by the director, Jerzy Gruza and Boleslaw Sulik, may have been embellished by the improvising leads but the foundations it sets ensure that one-of-a-kind *Deep End* remains far more than a time capsule. Yes, a Polish director shot a quintessentially British film largely in Germany, but the resulting pic still resonates today.

"I don't think it's dated at all," Asher explained while promoting the film's re-release. "But then it didn't fit its time even when it first came out."

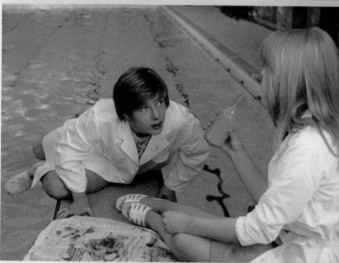

Jane Asher
Talks Deep End

While she is better known now for her prowess in the kitchen and her romance with Paul McCartney back in the days when Macca was known as the cute Beatle, in the '60s and '70s Jane Asher was building a career as a daring and versatile young actress.

As a child, she had appeared uncredited in Hammer's *The Quatermass Xperiment* (1955) before working on classic British TV shows like *Dixon of Dock Green*, *Dr. Finlays Casebook* and *The Saint*. On film, she featured in Disney's *The Prince and the Pauper* (1962) before Roger Corman cast her in *The Masque of the Red Death* (1964) with Vincent Price. She starred opposite a very cheeky and very cockney Michael Caine in Lewis Gilbert's cautionary tale *Alfie* (1966), before heading to Munich for Jerzy Skolimowski's stylishly grimy *Deep End* (1970) to deliver a firecracker performance that stole the film and redefined the Swinging decade for a '70s audience.

David Michael Brown spoke to the actress about playing the liberating and destructive Susan, a world-weary but groovy Londoner who has already seen too much in her young life…

DMB: You'd had made films like *The Buttercup Chain* and *Alfie* that encapsulated the sexual freedom of the '60s. *Deep End* offers a darker view of London at the tail end of the decade. What was it that attracted you to the project?

JA: It's a fantastic part, of course, and as soon as I read it, I knew it would be fun to make. The original screenplay was in rather peculiar English (at that stage, Jerzy's spoken English was very minimal) and in a way it added to the slightly surreal quality of the story. Generally, in my career, I've tended to play "nicer" characters on film, and some tough, cold ones on stage - no idea why! - and Susan combined the two which I could see would make her very interesting to play. In any case, how often do actresses get offered starring roles in films that actually have the backing

to get made? They're sure not to be turned down lightly!

DMB: What was it like working with Jerzy Skolimowski? Were you a fan of his work as a director?

JA: I only knew of him via his work on the screenplay of *Knife in the Water* - which was extremely well known and much admired at that time. Working with him was wonderful. He's a fascinating character - pretty serious and occasionally inscrutable. He's fastidiously tidy, which for someone like me, who has to struggle with natural untidiness, lent a certain frisson to everyday dealings. Even sitting in a restaurant, he would arrange the knives and forks, salt and pepper and so on as symmetrically as possible. (He told me after a week or so of working with him that when he had come round to my flat in London before filming to talk about costume, the sight of my shoes chucked in piles in the bottom of the wardrobe had horrified him. I'm glad he didn't let that put me off!

During filming, each evening he would set John [Moulder-Brown] and I the task of re-writing the next day's scenes to make them as colloquially English as we could. I've always felt that the fact the film was made with English and German actors, a Polish writer and director - and shot partly in the UK and partly in Germany - was a huge part of its dreamlike sense of otherness: not totally realistic but equally not just a fantasy. He encouraged our input all the time, and I spent many hours doing rewrites and colour coding my copy of the script to check the arc of Susan's story during the film.

DMB: Did you enjoy the freedom and improvisation he inspired on set?

JA: At first, we worked conventionally from the existing script, as worked on by all of us during the previous night's 'homework', but after a few days he encouraged John and I to improvise. I found it a bit unnerving at first, but once I got into it, I loved it. And it was worryingly easy to access my inner Susan, with her sarcasm and touch of cruelty. Hopefully, I left it on the set at the end of each day.

DMB: What was it like working with John Moulder-

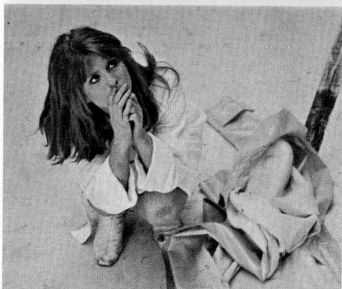

Brown?

JA: John and I bonded very easily and hugely enjoyed working with each other. He became a good friend and a confidante. When we were in Germany, which was the first place we filmed, we naturally tended to support each other as the only English participants at that stage.

DMB: Can you discuss collaborating with John on Susan's on-screen relationship with Mike?

JA: We seemed to slip into that relationship very easily: it was entirely acted of course - hopefully, I've never treated anyone quite as cruelly in real life - and our ways of approaching it seemed to blend easily. Jerzy was very clever at guiding us and encouraging us to try things. John's innocent young demeanour was so perfect, but in reality, he's far more knowing and in charge of himself than that.

DMB: What are your memories of filming in Munich?

JA: I can't remember much specifically. I know we started with the scene in the snow where I had to scrabble for the lost ring. I had met Jerzy in the UK of course when he first offered it to me and we chatted it all through and so on, but it was quite surreal suddenly being with an all-German crew and plunged straight into that scene for the first shots. But it was a very friendly and positive crew, especially the cameraman, Charlie [Steinberger]. He was wonderful and extremely supportive and, unlike Jerzy, the crew all spoke excellent English.

DMB: What do you remember about the Soho night shoots?

JA: I wasn't there as long as the rest of the cast and crew, but it all seemed to go very smoothly... I'm not quite sure that they actually had the correct permits - I seem to remember a bit of skulking around in certain areas so as

not to be spotted by the (real!) police.

DMB: Was it really you posing as 'Angelica'? I love the scene in the Underground where you and John argue about the poster.

JA: Yes - that's really me! When I filmed *The Masque of the Red Death* a few years earlier, I was extremely shy about nudity, and they stuck little round circles of material on my nipples in an attempt to preserve my modesty for the bath scene. They kept floating off in the water, of course, and the cameraman got more and more irritated by the constant stopping as I desperately fished around for them. By the time I made *Deep End*, I was far more relaxed, and Charly [Steinberger], the wonderful cameraman, made me feel very much at ease when he took the photographs for that cut-out 'stripper' picture. And for the naked section in the pool at the end of the film, I just went for it and trusted Jerzy to cut it together without it being too embarrassing. Nowadays I guess there'd be all sorts of consultants on set.

DMB: Looking back, what is your favourite memory working on *Deep End*?

JA: The fun we all had being together on the set - surprising ourselves when we made each other laugh with an unexpected or silly bit of improvising. And doing a take that Jerzy was happy with and praised. He was one of those directors, like a good teacher, who made you really want to please him.

DMB: Why do you think the film still resonates today?

JA: It still resonates with audiences because the characters are interesting and it's got a good story. That's what we all want to see, whatever the year and genre, isn't it?

If you can't
have the real thing—
you do all kinds of unreal things.

Paramount Pictures Presents in association with Maran Film and Kettledrum Productions

A Jerzy Skolimowski Film

"DEEP END" ®

Starring Jane Asher · John Moulder Brown · with Guest Star Diana Dors · Original music by Cat Stevens and the Can
Written by Jerzy Skolimowski · Executive Producer Judd Bernard · Produced by Helmut Jedele · Directed by Jerzy Skolimowski
Associate Producer Lutz Hengst · In Color · Distributed by Cinema International Corporation · A Paramount Pictures

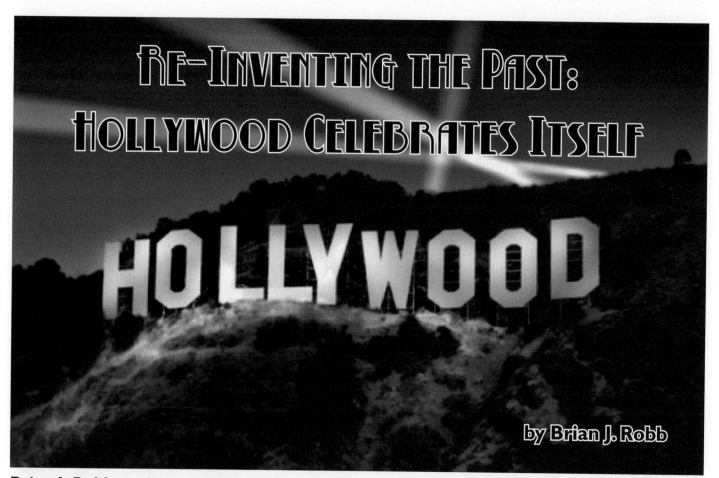

Re-Inventing the Past:
Hollywood Celebrates Itself

by Brian J. Robb

Brian J. Robb analyses '70s Hollywood's nostalgia for a long-gone era of moviemaking.

Hollywood in the '70s reached a new period of maturity. The film industry, which had properly developed as a business in the '20s with the formation of the classic Hollywood studios (MGM, Paramount, Warner Bros., 20th Century Fox, RKO and lesser players like United Artists and Columbia), was now 50 years old. Nostalgia kicked in, and Hollywood - an industry never shy about celebrating itself - began to look backwards. The so-called 'golden age' of Hollywood was when the studio production line system was at its peak, from the '20s to the start of the '60s when it began to unravel. At a time of huge uncertainty in the movie industry, there was nothing more comforting for filmmakers than to look back at where it all began.

In very different ways, both Peter Bogdanovich's *Nickelodeon* (1976) and Mel Brooks' *Silent Movie* (1976)

- both of which featured quintessential '70s star Burt Reynolds - celebrated the silent era of five decades before. Bogdanovich's film (co-written with W. D. Richter) was a faithful recreation of Hollywood's earliest days, beginning in 1914. Ryan O'Neal (reuniting with Bogdanovich following Depression-period comedy *Paper Moon*, 1973) stars as a lawyer Leo Harrigan caught up in the exciting business of picture making. Reynolds plays Buck, a would-be star and stuntman who teams up with Harrigan to make 'motion pictures'. Kathleen Cooke (Jane Hitchcock) is the actress who accidentally becomes a star and then comes between the two men.

Nickelodeon is an attractive recreation of the early days of filmmaking, when independent outfits fled to Hollywood to escape the attentions of Edison's Patents Company which set out, often violently, to 'protect' its assumed rights in filmmaking equipment. Bogdanovich based many of the incidents on stories told to him by original Hollywood figures he'd interviewed, including directors Allan Dwan, Raoul Walsh, Leo McCarey and John Ford.

Several rival projects celebrating silent movies were in the works in the early '70s, and Bogdanovich's ended up uncomfortably merged with a Columbia project called *Starlight Parade*, written by Richter. Brought in to direct, Bogdanovich reworked Richter's existing script to meet his own specifications - he wanted to include those 'real life' stories. He also wanted to make it in black and white (like his breakthrough *The Last Picture Show*, 1971, and *Paper Moon*). This led to a fight with the studio and a temporary cancellation of the picture.

Bogdanovich had wanted Jeff

Bridges (but ended up with O'Neal), John Ritter (but got Reynolds; Ritter remained in a smaller role) and his then girlfriend Cybil Shepherd (but got Hitchcock). In some ways, O'Neal and Reynolds played the wrong roles, which helped in their onscreen confusion. The fast-talking director may have suited Reynolds better, while O'Neal would be a more natural cross between Buster Keaton and Gary Cooper, which is how Reynolds played his largely slapstick role. O'Neal noted that Bogdanovich had rewritten what had originally been "a tough little script about Hollywood into a farcical series of precious little jokes." Despite that, this was a love letter to Old Hollywood, although it was a third flop in a row for Bogdanovich.

Mel Brooks' *Silent Movie* came at things from a different angle, being a then-contemporary silent movie about the struggle by a then-contemporary film director - Mel Funn (Brooks) - to make a modern silent movie in the style of the '20s. There is no spoken dialogue, relying instead upon '20s style intertitles (ironically, the only spoken word comes from mime artist Marcel Marceau). As well as aping silent movie style, Brooks went all-in on

a takedown of Hollywood, creating a satire about the way Hollywood operates. Funn wants to recruit big star names and his first target is *Nickelodeon*'s Reynolds, playing himself. Other stars include James Caan, Liza Minelli, Anne Bancroft (Brooks' wife) and Paul Newman. A clever balancing act sees Brooks pay tribute to the beginnings of the film business and create a takedown of some of its more egregious practices. More overtly comedic than *Nickelodeon*, *Silent Movie* is far less authentic, more concerned with getting in well aimed (and well deserved) digs at the film industry.

Although he missed out on *Nickelodeon*, Jeff Bridges starred in *Hearts of the West* (1975, released in Europe as *Hollywood Cowboy*) as

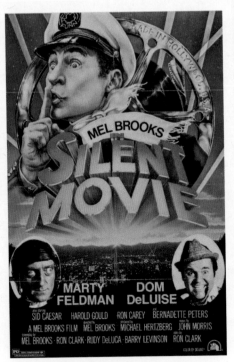

Lewis Tater, an aspiring novelist of '30s westerns (like Zane Grey) who instead finds himself cast as a leading man in B-movie cowboy pictures. Written by Rob Thompson and directed by Howard Zieff, *Hearts of the West* is a now generally forgotten production but was an efficient little comedy that helped Bridges on the road to stardom. Where it scores is in the depiction of B-western producers Tumbleweed Productions, echoing *Nickelodeon* in drawing laughs from the way movies were made in the early days. Among the supporting cast are Andy Griffith as a genuine old-time cowboy now playing bit parts, Alan Arkin as the unit manager who helps Tater's career and Blythe Danner as the script girl Tater falls for. Reviewing *Hearts of the West*, critic Roger Ebert dubbed it "a lovely little comedy" which saw Bridges "bring complexity to [his] role."

Dirty Movies

Also released in 1975 was *The Wild Party* (which shares its title with a 1929 Clara Bow silent movie). Set at the dawn of the talkies, James Ivory's film features James Coco as a silent era star Jolly Grimm, who's desperate to make a comeback. He throws a crazy party to screen his latest film hoping to rekindle studio interest, which turns into a

ribald bacchanalia when actor Dale Sword pursues Grimm's wife Queenie (Raquel Welch). Financed by exploitation house AIP, *The Wild Party* - as the character names suggest - was less than serious in intent. A troubled production (a period of re-editing followed poor test screenings), the reviews and box office were terrible, and it was quickly forgotten.

Also set in the early '30s, as movies made the painful switch to talkies, was *Inserts* (1975), starring Richard Dreyfuss (who'd just completed *Jaws*) as an agoraphobic director who ends up working in pornography (then known as 'stag films'). Like Ken Russell's later *Valentino*, John Byrum was able to depict scenes that would never have been seen in classic Hollywood cinema (Byrum would work uncredited on the *Valentino* script; Stephen Davies plays a Valentino type in *Inserts*). Veronica Cartwright plays a doomed, heroin-addicted fading starlet named Harlene (presumably after Jean Harlow, whose real name was Harlean Carpenter) whose squeaky voice is not suitable to sound, while Jessica Harper is Cathy Cake, an aspiring actress who has to double for the dead Harlene. After several filmmaking misadventures of an 'adult' nature, Dreyfuss' damaged director misses Clark Gable knocking on his door, hoping to hire him to direct his next picture. Shot in London on limited sets and filmed in near real-time, *Inserts* is an unusually frank take on the kind of events that must've happened in Old Hollywood, but which simply

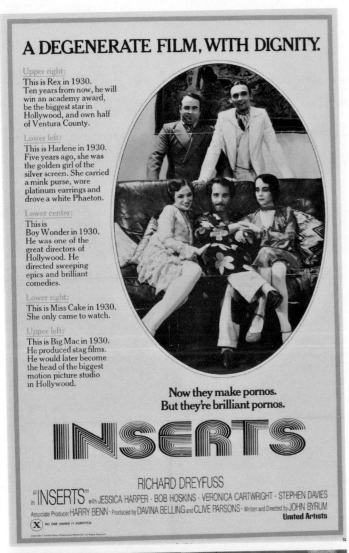

A DEGENERATE FILM, WITH DIGNITY.

Upper right:
This is Rex in 1930. Ten years from now, he will win an academy award, be the biggest star in Hollywood, and own half of Ventura County.

Lower left:
This is Harlene in 1930. Five years ago, she was the golden girl of the silver screen. She carried a mink purse, wore platinum earrings and drove a white Phaeton.

Lower center:
This is Boy Wonder in 1930. He was one of the great directors of Hollywood. He directed sweeping epics and brilliant comedies.

Lower right:
This is Miss Cake in 1930. She only came to watch.

Upper left:
This is Big Mac in 1930. He produced stag films. He would later become the head of the biggest motion picture studio in Hollywood.

Now they make pornos.
But they're brilliant pornos.

INSERTS

RICHARD DREYFUSS
in "INSERTS" with JESSICA HARPER · BOB HOSKINS · VERONICA CARTWRIGHT · STEPHEN DAVIES
Associate Producer HARRY BENN · Produced by DAVINA BELLING and CLIVE PARSONS · Written and Directed by JOHN BYRUM
X NO ONE UNDER 17 ADMITTED
United Artists

lights of Hollywood and 'The Last Tycoon' looking at the industry from the inside, chronicling the burnout of a top film producer.

In *The Day of the Locust*, William Atherton plays Ted, a Yale graduate who arrives in '30s Hollywood and becomes part of a diverse community of wannabes who all live in the same rundown apartment complex. These include aspiring actress Faye Greener (Karen Black), dwarf Abe Kusich (Billy Barty) and Mrs. Loomis (Gloria LeRoy) who hopes to turn her son (Jackie Earle Haley) into a child star. Also among them is one Homer Simpson (Donald Sutherland; just like 'Harry Potter' in 1986's *Troll*, this movie featured Homer long before *The Simpsons*!), a repressed accountant who has taken a fancy to Faye. There are parties and film screenings (including 'stag' films, as in *Inserts*), and Tod and Faye grow closer, sharing the same struggles to 'make it' as their lives weave in and out of the others. Things turn violent, with an unexpected death and a mob chase that turns into a riot leading to an apocalyptic inferno.

Although *The Day of the Locust* was considered a failure, it has been reassessed in the decades since. It depicts Old Hollywood as a brutal place, where even talented people struggle to succeed, and those on the margins are routinely badly treated. This was very much how West saw things, looking back from the '40s. It provides a contrast to the romantic nostalgia seen in Bogdanovich's picture.

BY TRAIN, BY CAR,
BY BUS, THEY CAME
TO HOLLYWOOD...
IN SEARCH
OF A DREAM.

THE DAY OF THE LOCUST
DONALD SUTHERLAND
KAREN BLACK
WILLIAM ATHERTON
BURGESS MEREDITH

could not be depicted on screen until the '70s and the end of the censorship of the long-lasting Production Code.

Two mid '70s movies that told cautionary tales of Old Hollywood were both based on novels written when the classic studio system was at its height. *The Day of the Locust* (1975), directed by John Schlesinger, was based upon the Nathanael West novel from 1939, while Elia Kazan's *The Last Tycoon* (1976) drew from F. Scott Fitzgerald's unfinished 1941 novel. Both books, coming at the subject from distinctive angles, charted the pitfalls of Hollywood, with 'The Day of the Locust' focusing on a group of would-be stars drawn by the deceptive bright

Some later critics even came to consider *The Day of the Locust* as more akin to a horror film in the way it tracks the downward spiral of its characters into desperate acts and seemingly divine punishment. Again, like several of the other films under consideration, this benefits from the freedoms of '70s cinema that those making films in the '30s could only dream of.

Coming at Hollywood from the top rather than the bottom, *The Last Tycoon*'s Monroe Stahr (Robert De Niro) was based upon Hollywood producer Irving Thalberg. He had one of the more dramatic rises and falls in Old Hollywood, beginning in the '20s as secretary to Universal Studio's boss Carl Laemmle. One of the notable projects

at Universal Thalberg was responsible for was 1923's *The Hunchback of Notre Dame*, starring Lon Chaney. He made his mark at MGM as production chief in the '30s, becoming known as Hollywood's 'boy wonder', devising a successful formula for movies and seeing the studio through the Depression. He married actress Norma Shearer and died in September 1936, aged just 37, due to complications from pneumonia.

F. Scott Fitzgerald began writing what became 'The Last Tycoon' in late 1939, just a year before his own death in late 1940, aged 44. The novel was intended as a fictionalised biography of Thalberg, with the 'boy wonder' lightly disguised as Monroe Stahr. In the movie, De Niro's Stahr is a lens through which Hollywood's 'golden age' of the '30s is refracted. Through his interactions with various departments and individuals at the studio, the film reveals the process behind film production in the '30s and '40s. Paralleling the industry story (in which he confronts a truculent union organiser played by Jack Nicholson) is a romance where Stahr becomes obsessed with troubled actress Kathleen Moore (Ingrid Boulting, herself related to the Boulting Brothers of British filmmaking fame). Representing classic Hollywood are Tony Curtis and Robert Mitchum, while others appearing include such '70s names as Theresa Russell, Anjelica Huston and Peter Strauss. Kazan's movie so captures the sepia look of Old Hollywood in all its art deco glory that it was rightly nominated for a Best Art Direction Oscar (losing out to *All the President's Men*).

Famous Faces

As well as direct representations of the era, there was also a '70s trend for biopics of famous classic Hollywood stars, kicked off by the double-bill of Sidney J. Furie's *Gable and Lombard* and Arthur Hiller's *W. C. Fields and Me*, originally released in February and March of 1976. Both quickly established a key trait of the era - a near total lack of historical veracity or accuracy to the real stories of those involved, beyond the broadest brush strokes, and the failure of '70s 'stars' to capture the personalities of Old Hollywood's finest performers.

A would-be screwball comedy (in the manner of the '40s movies) was an odd choice for Sidney J. Furie, director of *The Ipcress File* (1965) and *Lady Sing the Blues* (1972), in his attempt to recreate the romance between 'King of Hollywood' Gable and the then-married (to William Powell) Carole Lombard. James Brolin is fine as Gable until he

GABLE and LOMBARD

GABLE and LOMBARD

opens his mouth, and Jill Clayburgh's Lombard is played as a ditzy screwball heroine. Brolin and Clayburgh offer caricatures in the place of characters, barely scratching the surface of the lives of the stars they're portraying. Furie's film misses the mark as an account of old Hollywood-style filmmaking, with precious little time devoted to seeing these stars at work. Neither is the screenplay up to encapsulating the tragedy of Lombard's unexpected early death in a 1942 plane crash, returning from a War Bonds sales trip. The plane crash is used as a structuring device as Brolin's Gable waits to hear news of Lombard's fate.

Similarly inaccurate in historical detail and equally bizarrely cast, at least *W. C. Fields and Me* had a literary source: the 'tell all' book by Carlotta Monti, Fields' live-in secretary and romantic partner in the last years of his life. She's played by Valerie Perrine (after *The Day of the Locust*'s Karen Black turned it down), but unfortunately someone thought casting Rod Steiger as W. C. Fields was a good idea. It's a bizarre performance, weirdly convincing in some scenes and just utterly wrong in others. He's both impersonating the on-screen icon that was Fields while

endeavouring to capture something of the off-screen man (Mickey Rooney played Fields on stage around the same time, and might have been a better choice). There is another odd element in the form of John Marley playing Bannerman, the studio boss, maybe a nod to the role he'd earlier played in that notorious horse's head scene in *The Godfather* (1972).

There was an inherent problem with '70s actors attempting to embody icons of Old Hollywood: none of them seemed to have the necessary easy charisma. The nature of movie stars was very different in the '70s from the '40s. Figures like Gable and Fields were perhaps too larger-than-life to be embodied by the likes of Brolin or Steiger, talented though they surely were.

Even more difficult was any attempt

SHE WAS SOON TO BECOME THE GREATEST SEX SYMBOL
THE WORLD HAS EVER KNOWN.

A STIRLING GOLD PRESENTATION

STARRING
MISTY ROWE AS NORMA JEAN BAKER / CO-STARRING TERRENCE LOCKE / PATCH Mackenzie / PRESTON HANSON
MARTY ZAGON / ANDRE PHILIPPE / SCREENPLAY BY LYNN SHUBERT / LARRY BUCHANAN / DIRECTED BY LARRY BUCHANAN
MUSIC BY JOE BECK TITLE SONG WRITTEN BY JOHNNY CUNNINGHAM / PERFORMED BY THE SUNDOWN COMPANY
AN AUSTAMERICAN PRODUCTION TECHNISCOPE™ AND TECHNICOLOR®

along by the joie de vivre of Misty Rowe as the young Monroe. The exploitative nature and the low production values are compensated for by both Rowe's spirited performance (nowhere close to incarnating Monroe, but easily the highlight) and some out-of-time nascent feminism. 'Variety' noted of *Goodbye, Norma Jean*: "Misty Rowe … gives a fine and sensitive performance", while the 'Daily Express' noted that Rowe was "an actress, not a mimic." Although he pinched the title, Buchanan clearly couldn't afford to license the 1973 Elton John song. Buchanan and Rowe reunited for an '80s follow-up, *Goodnight, Sweet Marilyn* (1989).

The following year Buchanan churned out *Hughes and Harlow: Angels in Hell* (1977), where the formula is much the same. Chronicling the making of *Hell's Angels* (1930), the movie features Victor Holchak as Howard Hughes and Lindsay Bloom (from TV's *The Dukes of Hazzard*) as the doomed Jean Harlow. Noted the 'New York Times': "Neither Bloom nor Holchak are half as fascinating as the real-life characters they portray, and this, coupled with a stretched to the limit budget, results in a film that never quite reaches its potential."

Silent era icon Rudolph Valentino was depicted in a pair of contrasting films released in 1977: Ken Russell's *Valentino* and Gene Wilder's *The World's Greatest Lover*. These movies epitomised the standard approach to capturing Hollywood's past: the direct, if slightly satirical, history or

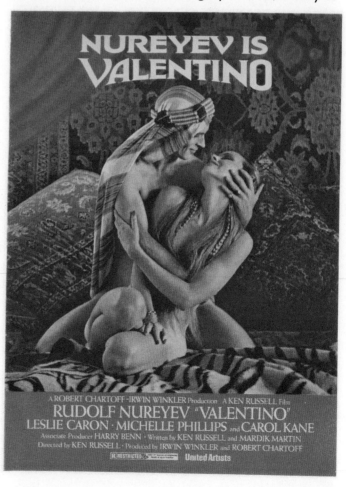

to capture a true Hollywood icon, one whose star persona surpassed that of the movies themselves. Weirdly, it fell to low-budget horror maestro Larry Buchanan to take the legend of Marilyn Monroe through the '70s. His Monroe picture, *Goodbye, Norma Jean* (1976), opens with Norma Jean Baker visiting a cinema in 1941 that is screening a news reel chronicling the romance between Gable and Lombard. Although the film has all the usual Buchanan trademarks - low budget, poor production values, dodgy performances, and general incompetence - it is carried

In his usual unrestrained over-the-top mode, Wilder plays a Milwaukee baker roped in to play a Valentino rival, 'Rudy Valentine', for a low-rent studio. Wilder was never as good on his own as he had been when working with Mel Brooks. *The Adventures of Sherlock Holmes' Smarter Brother* (1975) and *The World's Greatest Lover* were not a patch on the likes of *The Producers* (1967), *Blazing Saddles* (1974) and *Young Frankenstein* (1974), all of which starred Wilder under the direction of Brooks. Praised for its

the out-and-out slapstick spoof. *Valentino* arrived when Russell's career was swinging from critical acclaim (*Women in Love*, 1969) to critical disdain (*The Devils*, 1971). He'd been focusing on biopics, often of classical musicians, such as *The Music Lovers* (1971) about Tchaikovsky, *Mahler* (1974) and *Lisztomania* (1975), so the Valentino project seemed to fit. Flashing back from Valentino's death in 1926, the film chronicles his relationships with several women, as well as exploring his homosexuality. As well as Valentino, played by dancer Rudolph Nureyev, several other Old Hollywood characters appeared: Ali Nazimova (Leslie Caron), Natascha Rambova (The Mamas and the Papas' Michelle Phillips), studio moguls Joseph Schenck (David de Keyser) and Jesse Lasky (Huntz Hall, one of the original '30s 'Dead End Kids') and disgraced comedian Fatty Arbuckle (William Hootkins). There was a decent attempt at historical veracity in *Valentino* lacking in some other titles. It's easily the most serious of the '70s films looking back on the icons of Old Hollywood, serving to both celebrate an icon like Valentino while simultaneously deconstructing his star persona. Although a box office hit in Britain, Russell's *Valentino* failed to impress American audiences, flopping on release and receiving mixed reviews. Opulent and flamboyant, *Valentino* was part of a '70s vogue for all things '20s, in fashion (Biba was big), art (the return of the '20's 'new vision') and society (advances in social expression). Only in the '70s, though, could a movie be as explicit as Russell's *Valentino* on the sex and sexuality of the '20s.

Wilder's *The World's Greatest Lover* was entirely different.

period detail (not quite as finely realised as in *Valentino*), the film was criticised for its lack of comic appeal, with the 'Washington Post' noting: "the prevailing tone … is one of wretched excess, in both slapstick and sentimental passages." Certainly, 'excess' could be applied to Ken Russell's work, but it was of a different order than that of Wilder. Oddly, Carol Kane features in both Russell's *Valentino* and Wilder's *The World's Greatest Lover*.

Finally, in terms of 'straight' Old Hollywood biopics made in the '70s, there's the strangest of them all. *Won Ton Ton: The Dog Who Saved Hollywood* (1976) was directed, rather amazingly, by *Death Wish's* Michael Winner, and featured Bruce Dern and frequent Gene Wilder co-star Madeline Kahn. It's a biopic of a dog who became a '20s movie star, based upon the unlikely career of Rin Tin Tin, a German Shepherd who became a big star in silent movies. One of the dog's earliest films, 1923's *Where the North Begins*, was credited with saving Warner Bros. from bankruptcy. The original Rin Tin Tin lasted almost a decade in Hollywood, dying in 1932, only to be quickly replaced with a series of pooch performers that usurped his name.

Writer and producer Arnold Schulman intended for *Won Ton Ton* to be a satirical take on the Rin Tin Tin story, but Winner "directed with all the charm and wit of a chain-saw massacre." It's notable for returning to the source - after a fashion - by featuring as many original Old Hollywood performers as were still around in the mid '70s in cameos, including pre-code star Joan Blondell, musical star Alice Faye and Huntz Hall (also in *Valentino*). All this did was to point out the vast disparity between the 'real thing' and '70s imitators like Brolin, Steiger and Rowe. The 'Chicago Tribune' dubbed Winner's picture "a scattershot comedy that can't make up its mind whether to be 'wholesome family entertainment' or a smutty film industry in-joke. It goes both ways."

What had brought about this wholesale return to the past on the part of '70s Hollywood? There was, of course, the 50 years later aspect, a desire by a firmly established industry - one that had conquered the world - to look back at its own origins, to celebrate its own past successes. Many of the remaining stars of the silent era had begun to die off in the '60s and '70s, so it seemed a suitable time to explore where Hollywood had come from. This process had been helped by the arrival of the celebratory stage musical *Mack & Mabel* in 1974, chronicling the love story between Keystone Studio's king of comedy Mack Sennett and his leading lady, Mabel Normand, one of Hollywood's first female multi-hyphenate writer-director-producer-actor talents.

There is, however, a degree of uncertainty and

unease in this looking back on behalf of the picture business. Hollywood in the '70s had lost much of the certainty of the past. The hugely successful studio system, which perfected the production line process of creating successful movies in the '30s and '40s, had (for good or ill) been dismantled through the '60s. The rise of New Hollywood led to a degree of nostalgia for the era when things were more solid. Suddenly, in '70s Hollywood - to paraphrase the immortal words of William Goldman - nobody knew anything. From the turn of the decade to the arrival of '70s blockbusters like *Jaws* (1975), *Close Encounters of the Third Kind* (1977) and - most impactful - *Star Wars* (1977), Hollywood was somewhat adrift. Instead of forging a new way forward, some in that industry town began to look back, pining for an era long gone. While some films captured a perfectly valid nostalgia (*Nickelodeon*, *The Last Tycoon*), others - especially the star biopics - represented an egregious exhumation of a past they simply couldn't match any longer.

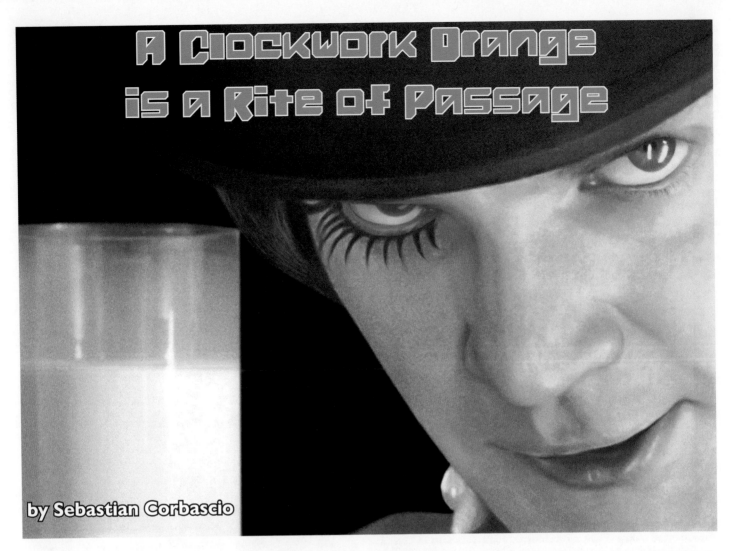

A Clockwork Orange is a Rite of Passage

by Sebastian Corbascio

"The belief that our children will reproduce us is what has kept the race going but seeing *A Clockwork Orange*, one's faith is blasted. From it, one brings away the fear that our children will kill us all."
Alexander Walker ('London Evening Standard')

On July 4th, 1973, 'The Times' reported that a 16-year-old boy had pleaded guilty at Oxford Crown Court to beating a 60-year-old tramp named David McManus to death and taking 1 and ½ pence from his body. Roger Gray, for the defence, told the court: "the link between this crime and sensational literature, particularly *A Clockwork Orange*, is established beyond reasonable doubt." In 1974, a gang of British youths attacked a teenage girl, singing *Singin' in the Rain* as they raped her (much like a scene from the screen version of *A Clockwork Orange*). In the years following, there were several more copycat crimes, leading a British judge to declare the film an "evil in itself."

In response to allegations that his movie was responsible for copycat violence, Kubrick stated: "to attribute powerful suggestive qualities to a film is at odds with the scientifically accepted view that, even after deep hypnosis in a posthypnotic state, people cannot be made to do things which are at odds with their nature."

And yet, strangely enough, it was withdrawn from British release at Kubrick's request. It had been running for 51 weeks in London's West End. No video copies could legitimately be sold or viewed in the UK from that point forth. A screening at the Scala Cinema in north London in 1993 led to prosecution. *A Clockwork Orange* wasn't shown theatrically in Britain until after Kubrick's death in 1999.

In the United States, it was nominated for four Academy Awards and won the New York Film Critics Circle Award for Best Picture. It was given an X-rating, though later Kubrick replaced approximately 30 seconds of sexually explicit footage to obtain an R-rating. The National Catholic Offices for Motion Pictures rated it C ('Condemned'), meaning Catholics were forbidden from watching it. *A Clockwork Orange* continues to appear on greatest of all time lists, usually around the high middle.

A Clockwork Orange is more than just a film, it's a rite of passage. Despite just turning 50, it still offends some and makes cinephiles of others. Either way, after one's first viewing one is never the same. It was originally intended to be made in the interim between *2001: A Space Odyssey*

and Kubrick's unrealized Napoleon project. Instead, it came between *2001* and *Barry Lyndon* on his filmography.

Many ingredients and themes make up the movie - Nasdat, the Ludovico Treatment, Switched-On classical, street gangs, free will, Pavlov, ultra-violence and much, much more are swirled into its dystopian, picaresque vision of a boy who becomes a machine.

The film was made a few years after *2001* had practically bankrupted MGM. Kubrick moved to Warner Brothers, where he was challenged to make a film on exactly one-sixth of *2001*'s $12-million budget. (*2001* had lost $800k in 1969 on its initial release, but recouped it thanks to a 1971 re-release). Kubrick was, in essence, being challenged to prove he could make a movie on a beer budget.

Alex DeLarge (Malcolm McDowell) speaks to us in Nasdat, the film's gangster-speak language, a goulash of Russian, Russian slang, cockney, some Roma expressions, and improvs by McDowell. The term 'clockwork orange' itself is cockney slang, meaning someone who works mechanically without free will. The film predicts that the Cold War ends and British and Russian youth cultures merge, coming up with their own rules and way of speaking (right down to a lingo that is almost incomprehensible and wallows in that glory). A lesser production, and a less courageous studio in less courageous times, might have insisted on translation subtitles (if they allowed Nasdat in the film at all). The reality is, though, that nowadays no studio would have the guts to go near *A Clockwork Orange* with a ten-foot pole.

The Droog (from the Russian word друг, meaning 'friend' or 'buddy') costumes, especially Alex's bowler hat and cane, are expressions of the British near-elites and professional classes. Their clothes are cricket uniforms (cricket being a British elite sport), made grotesque because the codpieces are being worn on the outside. Army issue boots are a nod to fascists and brownshirts. Kubrick was influenced by the Teddy Boys and other costumed English street gangs of the '60s and early '70s, and probably the street gangs in and around his home in the Bronx, New York.

The opening camera dolly reveals the Korova Milk Bar, with its black walls, balloon script drugged milk menu on the walls, naked women tables with dyed pubic hair and vaginas facing the camera, and hip clientele who like to drink with gangsters. We immediately understand that, in this cinematic universe, the club isn't some off-the-grid freak joint - it's mainstream.

Kubrick was always fascinated with genre. He would formulate a film according to what had come before, more often than not in the lowbrow cheapo realm. *The Killing* stems from noir/heist films; *2001: A Space Odyssey* is a product of the earth-meets-aliens genre; *Barry Lyndon* is a costume period drama; *The Shining* offers horror with more than a few Hammeresque flourishes; *Full Metal*

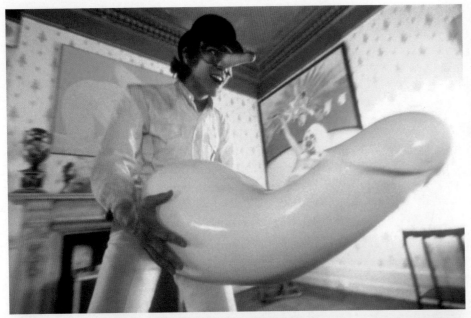

Jacket is basically an ode to World War Two flagwavers, updated and relocated to Vietnam; and *Eyes Wide Shut* is Kubrick's version of the soft-porn erotic thriller. *A Clockwork Orange* was inspired by AIP-Corman motorcycle pictures like *The Wild Angels* (1966). Make no mistake, it is an exploitation film - absolutely, completely and unapologetically. There was an avalanche of similar films - *Switchblade Sisters* and the like - before *A Clockwork Orange* came along. And there was no shortage of roving-gangs-outta-control films in the years that followed.

At the time of its production and release (1970-72), *A Clockwork Orange* rode a wave of films that came out of the wreckage of the Censorship Board and the introduction of the MPAA ratings system. The movie-going public couldn't get enough of Peter Fonda and Marilyn Chambers et. al. TV fare at the time was nice and safe, with family and police dramas which contained easy moralizing and tired social relevance, but the rest of the world wanted bikers, babes, heists, anti-heroes and an end to the goddamn war. The kids in America flashed peace signs but wanted onscreen heroes who liked to fuck shit up. In 1972, they got it with cockney flair and oodles of Beethoven from the same guy who'd made *2001: A Space Odyssey*. In the book 'A Cinema of Loneliness', Robert Phillip Kolker makes the point that Alex may well symbolize the authentic human (e.g. he acts human inside a technocracy populated by automatons).

Many critics have called *A Clockwork Orange* and *2001* companion pieces, speculating that while huge spaceships are orbiting above the Earth, the events of *A Clockwork Orange* are happening concurrently down on *terra firma*. An important scene which sets up that we are in the very near, very dystopian future is the one where a drunk (Paul Farrell) laments that mankind has put people on the moon yet cannot enforce proper law and order on earth. The scene comes just after Alex has asked: "what's so stinking about it

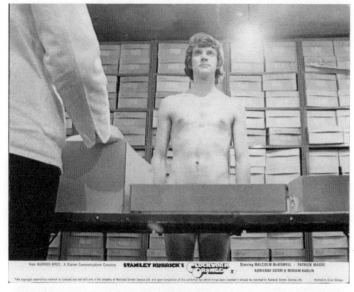

[the world]?" and seems really interested in what the man has to say, being a bit of a philosopher as well as a thug. Alex and his Droogs proceed to kick the crap out of the old drunk. They pummel him while he is on the ground, much like the apes in *2001* pummel their victim by the watering hole with their newly discovered implements.

Critics have also connected the Ape (or Moonwatcher as he's named in the '2001' novel) with Alex, noting how, despite advancements in modern technology and civilization, man hasn't really evolved much at all. In fact, Moonwatcher is like a friendly neighbor compared to Alex! Moonwatcher may use a bone to beat a competing tribe, but he does it to gain control of resources. Alex merely beats *his* victims for fun.

The derelict casino scene plays like something from a Mack Sennett slapstick silent film mixed with a bar brawl from a western. Feminist critics have pointed out that in this scene Kubrick is saying men find intimacy with each other in violence. That's why the Billyboy gang forget about the gang rape for the chance to battle their arch enemies. After the cowboy bar fight, the four Billyboys are on the ground, having been beaten and stomped by Alex's gang, which again harks back to the Dawn of Man beat-down from *2001*.

The home invasion and rape sequence, with *Singin' in the Rain* (an on-set improvisation by McDowell), is *A Clockwork Orange*'s tent pole scene. It is the scene most quoted and pantomimed by both nerds and nutters. Alex performs the *Singin' in the Rain* song and dance while beating and kicking the Alexanders, turning the invasion of their home into a vaudeville. He tells Mr. Alexander (Patrick Magee), while speaking directly into the camera, to: "viddy well, little brother, viddy well." It's like Alex is challenging us to look away, yet we can't. Without Alex singing *Singin' in the Rain*, the scene would just come across like dull, rapey porn. Kubrick dovetails the scene with a medium close-up of Mary Alexander (Adrienne Corri) clearly suffering.

A stark contrast with the rape bacchanal occurs in the next scene, when the Droogs return to the Korova Milk Bar for a nightcap. Dim (Warren Clarke) blows a raspberry at an opera singer while she belts out the choral from the *9th*, so Alex smacks his thigh with his staff, deeply offended at the way Dim "conducts himself public wise." It's as if Alex is perfectly OK with violent criminal behavior but breaching the rules of public decorum is entirely different. It conjures immediate and severe punishment from him, especially when the offender is interrupting Ludwig Van B! Alex raises his glass at the singer, and they lock eyes momentarily - first moves in a single's bar!

Beethoven's *9th Symphony* has a storied track record all its own. On one hand, it's considered the greatest single composition in classical (if not all) music. It's also a favorite of fascists, a sort of *We Will Rock You* for brownshirts. Its unselfconscious lack of subtlety, its cheerleading attitude toward human progress, make it the perfect anti-thesis of *Clockwork Orange*-era England. It's hard not to like. Its pastoral sentiment leaves nary a dry eye.

Alex comes home to what looks like a planned community, and like many planned housing communities it has gone to pot. Trash, graffiti and neglect rule. The location of the housing was an actual housing project - Southmere Estate in Thamesmead. As McDowell puts it,

it started out as a project built by the Labour government but in no time ended up a slum. For *A Clockwork Orange*, Kubrick selected buildings built in the Brutalist-style - monolithic, functional, seemingly ugly on purpose, the sort that would be favorites of Stalin.

Alex is visited by truant officer Mr. Deltoid (Aubrey Morris), and, in the grand tradition of noir coppers, Deltoid has a unique cadence to his lingo and an obsessive personality. Alex is the bee in Deltoid's bonnet; we hardly believe that he is on a mission to save Alex from himself, but he sets up what will come later during the Ludovico treatment scenes. "We have been studying the problem for damn near a century, but get no further with our studies. Is there some Devil that crawls inside of you?"

Indeed, it might be a Devil inside Alex, because he certainly shows little interest in the booty of his exploits. He throws that night's loot - a pile of stolen wristwatches, jewels and rolls of cash - into a drawer under his bed. They are mere trophies, souvenirs. His Droogs however, have a different *raison d'être* - Georgie (James Marcus) and Dim confront Alex and tell him they have rewritten the Droog mission statement. Less fun, more cash. Alex assures them they can have anything they want, so why complain? But in the next scene, he pummels the Droogs lakeside in glorious slo-mo, jumping up and down, grinning and snarling (another unsubtle nod to Moonwatcher from *2001*). Kubrick unveils the primates again.

Then there's the infamous Catlady scene which Kubrick chocks full of intellectual wankery: a woman with many cats ("pussies"), pre-Nagel art on the wall, Alex wearing his proboscis mask, and the erect penis sculpture which, in Alex's hands, becomes a murder weapon. There's enough in this single scene to fill a library of dissertations! The Catlady (Mariam Carlin) does yoga, phones the police on a princess phone, has an extravagant home, collects 'important' art - all the trappings of the British upper middle-class. She's cultured, bored and status driven. Note how she defends herself with a Beethoven bust, a very British version of a "momma with a shotgun protectin' her kin" (her kin being her cats and her status).

The hyper-stylization in *A Clockwork Orange* ends with Act One. Act Two marks an enormous tonal shift. The first act has a silent movie slapstick tone. Peril! Chases! Hijinks! The notorious undercranked sex scene with the two girls in Alex's bedroom recalls 18 frames-per-second silent movies with house piano accompaniment. Once the Second Act gets underway, even the sound changes. We get location noise - drips, air con, building hum - whereas previously, there was only Moog and practical sound hugging the dialogue. It could be argued the tonal shift is meant to represent the way Alex is no longer in control.

After Alex is "cured" of his criminal tendencies, we find ourselves asking what kind of evil this sociopath might perform with a powerful government behind him. The shot which wraps up the film - two naked women wrestling in confetti and being watched and applauded by Gilded Age era observers - implies a gateway to further things. It's a "to be continued..." moment. It can also be seen as a random shot thrown in before the end titles to make audiences and bonehead critics chase their tails. Alex's prison indoctrination is a clear jab at Britain - its pomp, its paperwork, its highly ritualized expression of state power. Even when the prison guard (Michael Bates) spreads Alex's glutes to check for contraband, the act is an extension of the Crown itself. The intake sequence is funny as hell, but features no music, only the hum of the fluorescent lights. The music reappears when the Minister (Anthony Sharp) visits the prison. Pomp and Circumstance - his music. He is the man in charge because he has a soundtrack.

After being selected to undergo the Ludovico treatment (an aversion technique which can supposedly rehabilitate even the worst criminals within two weeks), Alex is brought to the hospital. There's a hilarious receiving ritual involving multiple signatures on the paperwork. Music is back, and Alex thinks he's back in the driver's seat. The shock is that he is not. This becomes increasingly apparent after he has undergone the Ludovico treatment.

Technocracy has penetrated the medical establishment where quislings like Dr. Brodsky (Carl Duering) and Dr. Branom (Madge Ryan) seem to think a Pavlovian regimen can 'cure' evil. Beethoven's *9th* goes from being Alex's power theme to his albatross. The State penetrates even his marrow. It's no coincidence that Beethoven appears on the soundtrack of some of the film footage used during the Ludovico therapy. Brodsky comments that the music is "perhaps the punishment phase" of the treatment. Mind you, wouldn't being strapped to a chair, eyelids locked open, feeling like you're drowning, surely be punishment enough!

Later, Alex gets his just desserts from all the people he has harmed. These are the kind of pretentions found in fairy tales and Victorian picaresque tales. Kubrick is a picaresque director. After *A Clockwork Orange*, two of his films - *Barry Lyndon* and *Full Metal Jacket* - fit the picaresque definition: "Boy who's a bit pluckish starts a journey and has lots of adventures from which he barely escapes, only to return from whence he came, worse for wear but basically unchanged. Alex returns intact, and with a government post. He's cured, all right.

You can't really overstate McDowell's contribution to *A Clockwork Orange*. Kubrick on several occasions admitted he would have never made it without McDowell.

If he wasn't available, Kubrick would have just found a different project. McDowell enhanced the Nasdat with his improvisations (he even improvised *Singin' in the Rain* on the spot, which turns out to be a vital plot point). His brass bell voice and sonorous voice-over is singular. Matching an actor to role so perfectly only happens on a handful of occasions. McDowell has had more than a few excellent screen roles, but he can still draw a crowd when talking about *A Clockwork Orange* even though it's fifty years since its first theatrical run. If *that's* an albatross for him, only he can comment!

The odd thing about *A Clockwork Orange* is that its central theme - turning humans into machines via State power - never seems to really come up that much. When it does (e.g. the prison chaplain's two speeches defending human choice), it is completely impotent and falls on deaf ears. *A Clockwork Orange* explores more than just free will. Moreover, it isn't a philosophy symposium - it's a biker film!

A Clockwork Orange is great *because* it's great, a circuitous argument to be sure, but the lasting iconography, the might with which it wields influence, its endurance, and its status as a rite of passage for the cinematically inclined (and perhaps even a working stiff or two), have not diminished since its release. No-one had ever seen anything quite like it, and probably never will again. To quantify its staying power would be futile. Just enjoy it for the amazing work of art it is.

The Muppet Movie

by Kevin Nickelson

Would the Most Sensational, Inspirational, Celebrational, Muppetational series on TV be the same on the big screen?

"The Muppets are so innocent and positive in a world that is pretty cynical and at times pretty negative and bitter. They bring something that audiences love and want" (James Frawley, director of *The Muppet Movie*)

Having been a success for years on television, the concern of Muppets creator Jim Henson in bringing the beloved puppet characters to the big screen was not so much whether audiences would accept them but whether the aesthetic of meshing them with real-world locations would work. James Frawley, hired by Henson to helm the Muppets' debut feature, agreed with the master puppeteer. The director explained, in a 2014 interview with Beth Roessner for USAtoday.com: "The question was, since the Muppets had only been photographed on tape inside the studio, would they be accepted in a real location? Could you believe a frog and a pig in the real world?"[1] Henson, Frawley and Frank Oz decided to do something somewhat unusual by screen-testing some of the characters in actual London locations (the series was being shot in England at the time). "We shot them in and amongst cows, trees, farmland and cars to see if you accepted *their* reality mixed in with *real* reality," Frawley added. "It was also way for Jim to see how I worked with them and if I understood the process, which I didn't at the beginning."

Filming was completed in 87 days. It turned out to be more arduous to shoot than some of the biggest budgeted live action-adventure pics before or since. The process of incorporating the fabric-created puppets, invisible puppeteers, flesh-and-blood actors and actual sets/locations into one scene as seamlessly as possible was extremely challenging. Filming took place in Los Angeles, where soundstages were built. "They could be taken up in sections," explained Frawley. "Every scene was shot through the camera, and no effects were added later. When five or six Muppets crossed the stage in a group to approach Orson Welles in his office, it's actually five or six guys on a dolly being wheeled across the stage. So, what you have to do is frame things in the foreground - sofas and chairs - so you didn't see below the frame."

According to the Muppet Show Fan Club Newsletter, the Florida swamp scene early in the picture was accomplished by Henson squeezing himself into a special metal container rigged with an air hose (for breathing) and a rubber glove extending from a hole in the top. He then lowered himself into a water tank, then under the water, under the log, and even under Kermit! If you thought Fozzie was actually driving his car later on, think again. The whole sequence involved a diminutive actor hidden in the trunk, driving remotely with a TV monitor to assist and puppeteers crouched in the seats or on the floor. The first attempt to film this sequence nearly failed because, just as the director yelled "Action", the monitor blinked and an assistant director with a walkie-talkie had to talk the hidden driver through the manoeuvres one step at a time. Even more ambitious was the final shot of the film, which features 250 different Muppets and 150 puppeteers.

A six-foot deep, seventeen-foot wide pit was constructed to hold the artists, who were hired from the Los Angeles Guild of the Puppeteers of America.

One of the co-stars of the feature, Austin Pendleton (playing the character Max), had a less than harmonious take regarding life on set. "It was a very unhappy set, because Jim [Frawley] was very unhappy directing the movie. And I noticed that was the only time the Muppet people used an outside person to direct a Muppet movie. They never did that again. After that, it was either Jim Henson or Frank Oz. And I would have liked to have been in one of those, because those sets were very harmonious. But this was not. All my scenes were with Charlie Durning, whom I already knew, because he had a part in *Fiddler on the Roof* when I was in it, but his part got eliminated. We got to know each other during that. And now, of course, he's having quite a film career. So, at the L.A. airport, just after we were through with *The Muppet Movie*, on my way back to New York, I called Charlie from the airport and said: 'I loved working with you, and I don't know how I would have gotten through that movie without you.' Just hanging out with him really pulled it together for me. He said: 'Well, we can hang out some more, because I'm about to

"THE MUPPET MOVIE"
© 1979 Associated Film Distribution (AFD)

go to New York and do a film.' I asked what, and he said: 'An Alan J. Pakula film.' I said: 'Oh fuck, you lucky dog.' And so, he said he'd get me into the film, and he did. It was that Alan Pakula movie with Burt Reynolds (*Starting Over*)."

Dave Goelz, the man behind such iconic Muppets as the Great Gonzo and Dr. Bunsen Honeydew, had his own thoughts about the transferal of Henson's world from small screen to the big screen. He discussed the way the film reflects on the creator of this magic realm, Henson himself. "Because of the global success of the characters on television, we knew the public was hungry for them, but we didn't know if the onscreen experiment would work.

We didn't know if people would accept them the same way if they were out in the real world like they were in this movie. The characters pulled the audience in, moved the story along. They made it work, and it was still all about the characters. Do you know what the most interesting thing about *The Muppet Movie* is to me, still to this day? If you want to get some sense of Jim Henson, watch that movie because Kermit is so much like Jim. Longtime colleague Jerry Juhl wrote it, and he knew Jim very well."

Juhl was brought in to work on Henson's first TV show *Sam and Friends* in 1955 and stayed connected with the Muppets, in one form or another, right through to 1999's *Muppets in Space*. He co-wrote the first film with Jack Burns and was partly instrumental in the meta-humor style of the picture, as well as the way characters occasionally break the fourth wall (a still rather unique gimmick in 1979, and one which works well). A key reason for the success of this first silver screen entry is that dynamic relationship between Juhl and Henson, which comes across on celluloid. When it came to the question of any divide between the man and his vocation, Juhl really pegged Henson's personality in comments he made to Brian Jay Jones for the 2013 book 'Jim Henson: The Biography'. "Everything was play for him. *Work* was play." Jones also quoted another director who had worked on *The Muppet Show* on television, who said

that whenever he tried to make suggestions to Henson after a take, Henson's reply would always be: "Just talk to Kermit."

The 8-million-dollar budgeted movie ended up a box office bonanza, taking in over $65-million in the U.S. and Canada alone. It remained the highest grossing puppet film until 2011's *The Muppets*. There have been a few theories over the years about why it was so popular on release (and, indeed, why it remains so to this day). The immense star roster of cameos (Bob Hope, James Coburn, Richard Pryor, Telly Savalas, Orson Welles, Edgar Bergen, Mel Brooks, Elliot Goud, Milton Berle, Charlie McCarthy and many others) is one explanation. The writing, with its pointed humor, by Juhl and Burns is a hypothesis which also frequently springs up. Dave Goelz strips it down to something simpler still. He felt *The Muppet Movie* was a hit because Kermit's journey from the lily ponds of a Florida swamp to Hollywood glitz mirrored the rise of Henson himself, and the public seem to love a good rags-to-riches tale. "It was very much like Jim. We always felt that Jim was on a journey to put something positive into the world and make the world a little bit better place. That was his underlying philosophy, and it was there under every single thing we ever did. Jim always believed there was enough for everybody. Even in a business deal, he wanted both sides to profit. Jim didn't have a win-lose mentality. He celebrated diversity, different cultures of the world, and how they enrich each other. He was very wise. He acted in good faith with people all the time and with generosity. It was almost always returned."

And that's definitely what the world needs now, more than ever. More people like Jim Henson... and more Muppets. Many more Muppets!

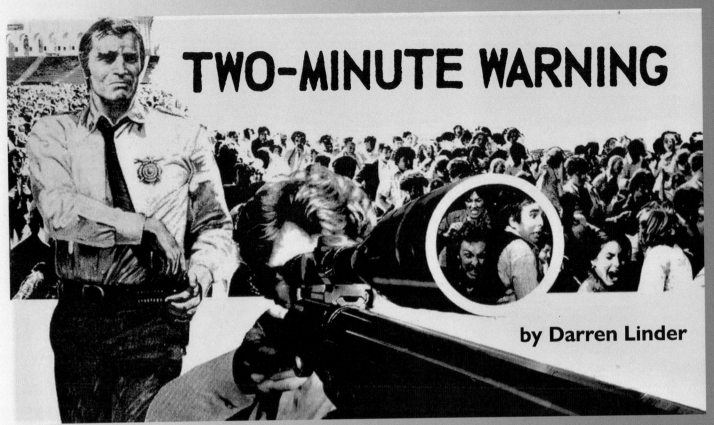

TWO-MINUTE WARNING

by Darren Linder

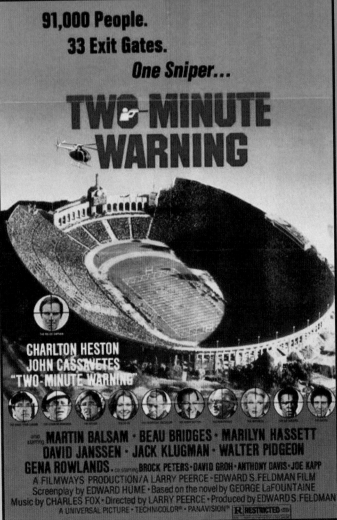

91,000 People.
33 Exit Gates.
One Sniper...

TWO-MINUTE WARNING

CHARLTON HESTON
JOHN CASSAVETES
"TWO-MINUTE WARNING"

also
starring MARTIN BALSAM · BEAU BRIDGES · MARILYN HASSETT
DAVID JANSSEN · JACK KLUGMAN · WALTER PIDGEON
GENA ROWLANDS co-starring BROCK PETERS · DAVID GROH · ANTHONY DAVIS · JOE KAPP
A FILMWAYS PRODUCTION/A LARRY PEERCE - EDWARD S. FELDMAN FILM
Screenplay by EDWARD HUME · Based on the novel by GEORGE LaFOUNTAINE
Music by CHARLES FOX · Directed by LARRY PEERCE · Produced by EDWARD S. FELDMAN
A UNIVERSAL PICTURE · TECHNICOLOR® · PANAVISION® [R] RESTRICTED

Two-Minute Warning is an engaging thriller from 1976 starring Charlton Heston, John Cassavetes and an anonymous sniper at the Super Bowl. This film brilliantly focuses on two huge American obsessions: football and guns. It rode on the coattails of some of the most successful disaster films of the early '70s, including the holy trinity of *Airport*, *The Poseidon Adventure* and *The Towering Inferno*.

While this film certainly doesn't belong in the pantheon of '70s classics from Scorsese or Coppola, I consider it much better than it is given credit for and deserving of another look. Highlights include great dramatic soundtrack music, a fantastic cast, point of view camerawork reminiscent of stalker/slasher horror films, use of a split diopter lens, realistic blood squibs, and truly impressive crowd panic

scenes once the murderous pandemonium begins.

In 1968, Peter Bogdonavich released a film about a sniper murdering strangers called *Targets*. That may have been the first movie to delve into this taboo subject. Both *Targets* and *Two-Minute Warning* likely were influenced by the true-life events of Charles Whitman in 1966, known as the Texas Tower Sniper. He shot at people for about 90 minutes from a clock tower, killing 16 and wounding 31 others before being shot to death by police officers.

Director Larry Peerce took this premise and put it in one of America's most beloved and highly attended sporting events, the Super Bowl. We are given very little background on the sniper, but we follow him in first-person POV moving camera shots. Later, as he is positioned in an isolated perch under the scoreboard, we view possible targets in the crowd and on the field with him. Viewing the potential victims through the crosshairs of his rifle scope, we become complicit - we *are* the shooter. There are several shots where the camera is scanning the crowd and the rifle is brought up into the frame, seamlessly shifting to look through the scope at a zoomed-in close-up view of a person. This exact shot has been emulated in every first-person shooter video game from *Call of Duty* to *Halo*. According to the director's commentary, it required building a special housing that could be locked onto the camera and brought into and out of the frame, adjusting for the perspective and focus change without any edits.

Charlton Heston is perfect for the role of the Police Captain trying to control an uncontrollable situation. Honestly though, he isn't given much to do for the first hour, and doesn't have much dialogue. It made me wonder if they'd had to cut out other footage of his character for time concerns. John Cassavetes plays the SWAT team commander. Yes, THAT John Cassavetes, the independent film director of such unique and improvisational '70s movies as *A Woman Under the Influence*, *Opening Night*, *Husbands* and *The Killing of a Chinese Bookie*. I was shocked to see him in the role of a family man who becomes an absolute badass when he goes to work.

I read the book by George LaFountaine so I could compare it to the film. The book starts out with a great scene that was pushed further back in the film. It's the scene where the live television camera truck crew is constantly chattering over the dozens of monitors. When they patch into the feed from the Goodyear Blimp overhead, the

camera catches sight of a man up on the scoreboard tower who shouldn't be there, especially since he has a gun next to him. The film should have started with this scene, but instead it begins with opening shots of the empty football stadium in the early morning, making it seem like a revered holy temple, later to be filled by thousands of spectators for the violent games to follow. Then they added a scene of the sniper practicing by randomly shooting a man on a bicycle from a hotel window.

Another huge change from the book is the elimination of the sniper's horrific backstory. In the book, the author ticks off all the boxes of things that supposedly might psychologically contribute to his developing antisocial/psychotic behavior. We suffer through grisly flashbacks involving childhood accidental death by a firearm, parental alcoholism and severe child abuse, animal torture and killing, homosexual shaming, heterosexual failure and shaming, a suicide attempt, parental death, foster homes, etc. In trying to somehow explain the origins for the homicidal shooter we lose our way and perhaps even feel some sympathy for him, which certainly was not the intent of the book. The film works so much better without dealing with the man's history at all. We learn nothing about him. We don't know anything about his political leanings or childhood trauma, and we don't need to.

I am reminded of this very applicable quote from the 1986 serial killer film *Manhunter*:

"*As a child, my heart bleeds for him. Someone took a little boy and turned him into a monster. But as an adult… as an adult he's irredeemable. He butchers whole families to fulfill some sick fantasy. As an adult, I think someone should blow the sick fuck out of his socks.*"

There is also a very different version of the film that, unfortunately, was shown often on television. Studio executives, in all their wisdom, decided to shoot an entirely new subplot involving an art gallery heist for the television premiere. The sniper in the football stadium was to be a distraction and decoy. The idea of a homicidal sniper acting alone with no motivation made them uncomfortable. They added in about 45 minutes of this new nonsensical subplot while removing 45 minutes of the original film. This takes away all of the power of the original story and makes a terrible movie. If this is the only version that you've seen, I strongly recommend watching the theatrical film. All DVD and Blu-Ray editions are the preferred theatrical version. The Shout! Factory Blu-ray released in 2016 does include the terrible TV re-edit as an extra feature. Movie theaters also concocted a gimmick where they would not allow anyone to enter the theater after the two-minute warning was given in the football game in the movie. Bright red posters in the cinema were put up announcing this.

out of his bag, reaches up around the scaffolding platform and yanks the kid down to the ground. He then stomps him in the middle of his back and zip ties his hands together. It's a great tense little scene made more impactful by having a famous director play the character. It reminds me of Spielberg using French New Wave director Francois Truffaut in a role in *Close Encounters of the Third Kind*.

The rest of the cast is equally great, in roles of varying complexity and importance. Gena Rowlands, who was married to Cassavetes for 25 years, is great. Jack Klugman, Beau Bridges, Martin Balsam, David Janssen, Walter Pidgeon, and several other familiar faces from '70s movies bring normalcy and realism to the story. However, learning all of the backstories to these characters wasn't as necessary. The film would have been more streamlined and tense if they perhaps skipped or shortened some of these subplots. We follow a football player with a potential injury, a man with huge gambling debts betting on the game, a pickpocket team, a regular family with kids and financial challenges, a minister, a couple with marital problems, etc. This all is meant to make us care more about the characters and fear for their death from the sniper. But it often feels like slightly unnecessary melodrama. I actually

It is interesting hearing the SWAT team hypothesize about who might be the shooter's intended target, since it couldn't possibly just be random murder. They wonder if the shooter might be targeting a particular football player or a coach. They discuss the VIPs and decide to evacuate them quietly, them being society's purported elite. They identify, locate and escort out the upper echelon of attending Governors, Senators, two astronauts and an Arab oil prince, They, of course, call off the Presidential motorcade that was on the way there at half-time. The hoi polloi are not warned of the danger and are allowed to stay. Classism at it's finest.

My favorite scene is when the SWAT team notice a teenager has climbed up onto a higher platform to observe the game. Since they are trying to maintain tactical positions around the sniper, having anyone out of place (or potentially drawing attention to their agents who are also positioned in the lighting towers) would need to be squelched. The kid is also making himself a more potential target of the sniper. But they suspect that he may be an accomplice since he has duffle bag with him. Cassavetes, in plainclothes, positions himself near the teenager while another agent disguised as a peanut vendor verbally engages him asking him to get down. When the teenager rudely refuses to get down, Cassavetes calmly pulls an Uzi

91,000 People... 33 Exit Gates...
One Sniper...

TWO·MINUTE WARNING

CHARLTON HESTON
JOHN CASSAVETES
"TWO-MINUTE WARNING"
also starring MARTIN BALSAM · BEAU BRIDGES · MARILYN HASSETT · DAVID JANSSEN
JACK KLUGMAN · WALTER PIDGEON · GENA ROWLANDS
co starring BROCK PETERS·DAVID GROH·ANTHONY DAVIS·JOE KAPP
A FILMWAYS PRODUCTION/A LARRY PEERCE · EDWARD S.FELDMAN Film
Screenplay by EDWARD HUME · Based on the novel by GEORGE LaFOUNTAINE
Music by CHARLES FOX · Directed by LARRY PEERCE · Produced by EDWARD S.FELDMAN
A UNIVERSAL PICTURE TECHNICOLOR® · PANAVISION® DISTRIBUTED BY CINEMA INTERNATIONAL CORPORATION

would have liked more backstory on the Heston character, since we get none, and the Cassavetes character.

The film really ramps up about an hour in, as the tactical team is aware of the sniper and doing everything that they can to mitigate this threat. When the shooting finally starts, the pandemonium captured on film is riveting and shocking. The crowd panic and stampede scenes are masterfully done. Realistic and explosive blood squibs are used to great effect. Managing that many extras on film is impressive to watch, especially since so many modern directors opt for CGI when large groups of people are needed. Our eyes have become accustomed to watching huge crowd scenes done with CGI, so when we see an actual crowd of real human beings charging across a football field towards the players, it hits differently. The shots of the crowd crushing towards exits and trampling each other are so well done that it feels like a documentary. The director talks about the filming of these scenes in the commentary track, saying they were managing up to 3000 extras. That realism makes the entire movie work.

This finale - where the SWAT team is trying to move in, minimize losses and take out the sniper - is as tense and gripping as any other '70s action set piece. We are rooting for the characters that we have grown to care about to survive. As the sniper plugs away at innocent people and exchanges fire with the SWAT team, a SWAT spotter from up in the Goodyear Blimp itself starts shooting down at him. This sequence is the best part of the film, and is truly a sight to behold.

Watching *Two-Minute Warning* almost 50 years after it was released, I appreciated the little touches and differences. For example, football games in the '70s didn't require you to walk through metal detectors or have your bags searched, two measures commonly done to prevent guns from entering large crowd venues. The Beau Bridges character drives past a parking lot and comments about how charging $5 for parking is absolutely out of line. The Heston character references "the stabbing at Altamont", which is a reference to the 1969 incident at the Rolling Stones concert where a man was stabbed to death by Hell's Angels staff who were working as security. And of course, the biggest change was that nobody in the crowd was filming the game or themselves on their smart phones.

As someone who works in the security field doing large events and crowd control, I was fascinated by the behind-the-scenes machinations of the SWAT team and other agencies. Acting as a liaison between different organizations with different strategies on handling an emergency was familiar to me. I appreciated their accurate radio communication and their efforts to quietly stage a response secretly to avoid a panic. Dealing with a crowd so large that, if they rioted, so much damage and death would happen. Trying to keep collateral damage low, safely evacuate people, and connect injured victims with medical staff. Preparing for pandemonium in an active shooter scenario played out on celluloid.

It is challenging to watch this film since we now live in a society in America where mass shootings are far more common. In 1976, the film was criticized for being too unbelievable and preposterous. In 2021, there were more mass shootings in America than there were days in the year.

At the end of the film, John Cassavetes gets to speak my favorite lines in the screenplay. It's a very prophetic monologue about the nature of post-incident media analysis and societal fixation on the carnage.

"You'll be hearing a lot more about him on television for the next couple of weeks. Where he went to school... his nice Mom... his pet dog... his old gym teacher... the body count... and how the cops really didn't have to kill him."

ULZANA'S RAID

A Bloody Masterpiece

by James Lecky

The image of the U.S cavalry riding to the rescue is central to the popular conception of the Hollywood western. In John Ford's ground-breaking *Stagecoach* (1939), it is the cavalry who, just when all seems lost, deliver the coup de grace to Geronimo's marauding war-party, an image repeated and echoed (sometimes distorted) in the cinematic history of the west.

The 'cavalry western' became something of a mainstay in Hollywood, from Michael Curtiz's *They Died with Their Boots On* (1941) - a highly romanticised version of the life and death of George Armstrong Custer - through countless B pictures in the '50s, to the harder-edged fare of the '60s and '70s like Sam Peckinpah's *Major Dundee* (1965), Ralph Nelson's *Duel at Diablo* (1966) and *Soldier Blue* (1970), up to 2017's *Hostiles*.

It perhaps goes without saying that the sub-genre found its best-known expression in Ford's westerns, in particular his celebrated cavalry trilogy of *Fort Apache* (1948), *She Wore a Yellow Ribbon* (1949) and *Rio Grande* (1950), as well as *Sergeant Rutledge* (1960) and his swansong western *Cheyenne Autumn* (1964).

Inevitably, the cavalry western brings with it a certain amount of cultural baggage - the Thin Blue Line attempting to impose order on a barbaric land, notions of Manifest Destiny, a rose-tinted view of America's colonial past and, in particular, a "white man good, red man bad" worldview espoused in films that were, more often than not, designed to do nothing more than entertain.

Nelson's *Soldier Blue* flipped the cavalry trope, presenting the U.S cavalry as rapacious and brutal, a "red man good, white man bad" viewpoint that also runs through Arthur Penn's *Little Big Man* (1970) and Kevin Costner's *Dances with Wolves* (1990).

Robert Aldrich's *Ulzana's Raid* repudiates all such notions and imagery in one brutal fell swoop, steadfastly refusing to take either stance.

Arizona in the 1880s: a group of Chiricahua Apache break free from the San Carlos reservation. Their leader, Ulzana (Joaquín Martínez), is determined to regain his lost power with the help of a murderous war party. Lt. Garnett DeBuin (Bruce Davison) is charged with bringing them back and preventing bloodshed. He is aided by ageing scout McIntosh (Burt Lancaster) and Apache tracker Ke-Ni-Tay (Jorge Luke). Like Conrad's 'Heart of Darkness' (1899), the pursuit leads to violence and horror from which no one emerges unchanged or unscathed.

A filmmaker of remarkable scope and versatility, Aldrich's influence was profoundly felt in Europe. *Vera Cruz* (1954) helped to define the loose morality of the spaghetti western, *The Dirty Dozen* (1967) spawned the macaroni combat subgenre of European war films, and *What Ever Happened to Baby Jane?* (1962) more or less created the hagsploitation/psychobiddy genre often mined by Hammer in the '60s. By the early '70s, following a series of commercial (although not artistic) failures - including *The Killing of Sister George* (1968), *Too Late the Hero* (1970) and *The Grissom Gang* (1971) - his star was on the wane and Aldrich took a massive cut in his usual fee to direct *Ulzana's Raid*.

Burt Lancaster was one of the great post-war stars

of Hollywood, a consummate screen actor who quickly graduated from matinee idol to more complex work such as *The Sweet Smell of Success* (1957), *Elmer Gantry* (1960), *The Leopard* (1963) and *The Swimmer* (1968). He had worked with Aldrich before, on the aforementioned *Vera Cruz* and *Apache* (both 1954). *Apache* might be thought of as a proto-revisionist western and was one of the first to put a human face on the Native Indian, hitherto a constant villain in American westerns. In it, Lancaster played Massai, a Chiricahua who conducts a one-man war of resistance but ultimately has no choice but to return to 'civilised' society (or, in other words, the reservation).

In some ways, Ulzana might be thought of as Massai grown old and bitter. Once a powerful warrior, his power has grown thin. As Ke-Ni-Tay explains: "Ulzana is long time in the agency. His power very thin. Smell in his nose is old smell of the agency. Old smell. Smell of woman, smell of dog, smell of children. Man with old smell in the nose is old man. Ulzana came loose for new smell - pony running, the smell of burning, the smell of bullet. For power!"

Alan Sharp's screenplay is lean and efficient, balancing introspective moments with scenes of extreme violence, giving voice to both the Apache and cavalry. DeBuin cannot understand Ulzana's cruelty, ("Could you kill a man like that?") but for Ke-Ni-Tay, it is a cultural norm ("Here, in this land, man must have power.") McIntosh is a pragmatist - when asked if he hates the Apache, he replies: "That'd be like hating the desert 'cause there ain't no water in it. For now, I can get by just being plenty scared of 'em."

Lancaster is magnificent in *Ulzana's Raid* - one of a late-career trio of westerns that also includes *Lawman* and *Valdez is Coming* (both 1971) - older than his prime, of course, but still lithe and pantherish in his movements. More than that, he is deliberately monolithic, revealing little, yet simultaneously eloquent in his stillness.

Sharp's screenplay was initially conceived as a homage to John Ford, but the end result could not be further removed, unless by deliberate parody (such as Richard Mulligan's beautifully insane performance in *Little Big Man*). Aldrich's landscape is not that of Monument Valley, but rather harsh scrub and hard desert. His protagonists are not ambitious officers, drunkenly charming sergeant-majors or comical foreigners. They are rather naïve young men and hard-bitten veterans, guys trying to survive with a modicum of their honour intact. His violence is often extreme, visceral and seemingly pointless.

By the '70s, the western was in crisis. In the early days of Hollywood, the audience was familiar with the cinematic landscape and prepared to accept a heroic version of the past. But by the '50s, following the Second World War, the genre developed a certain cynicism, best exemplified by the westerns of Anthony Mann and Budd Boetticher, before moving as a popular form to television. The success

One man alone
understood the savagery
of the early American
west from both sides.

BURT
LANCASTER
in
ULZANA'S
RAID

co-starring
BRUCE DAVISON   RICHARD JAECKEL

Music by FRANK DeVOL · Written by ALAN SHARP · Directed by ROBERT ALDRICH · Produced by CARTER DeHAVEN
A CARTER DeHAVEN-ROBERT ALDRICH PRODUCTION · A UNIVERSAL PICTURE · TECHNICOLOR®

of Sergio Leone's *A Fistful of Dollars* (1964) led to something of a renaissance in the form, particularly in Europe. Hollywood naturally reacted, and the American western gained a harder edge.

Ulzana's Raid is violent. Its depiction of torture, death, rape and the aftermath is graphic but never gratuitous and never for the sake of entertainment. Aldrich delivers his hardest blows early on - a woman is shot between the eyes to save her from gang rape by a soldier who, moments later, blows his own brains out rather than face capture and torture; Rukeyser (Karl Swenson), a gruff but loving farmer, is tortured to death with his dead dog's tail stuffed into his mouth; organs are ripped from corpses and thrown around as playthings. But, deliberately, the nature of the violence becomes more cinematically conventional as the film progresses, less explicit, as though through repetition violence has become the norm and its portrayal and aftermath are inconsequential. Both Ulzana and McIntosh die off-screen, the latter in an iconic freeze-frame with Lancaster leonine and stoic in the face of death.

Much has been made, of course, about the parallels in *Ulzana's Raid* with the then-ongoing Vietnam War - the 'civilized' U.S forces against an 'uncivilized' indigenous population - but at some fifty years removed, its themes seem as much a comment on the western itself as on contemporary global politics.

The landscapes of Ford and Leone's westerns were often beautifully shot (e.g. *The Searchers* [1956] and *Once Upon a Time in the West* [1968]), to the extent where they often became a silent but evocative cinematic character in their own right. Rarely, except in the desert sequences of *The Good, the Bad and the Ugly* (1966), was the backdrop a deadly one.

The landscapes of *Ulzana's Raid* are different, if no less beautifully lensed by cinematographer Joseph Biroc, a frequent Aldrich collaborator. They are for the most part arid and hostile, places of ambush rather than refuge, hardly fit for human habitation. This view is foreshadowed in a conversation earlier in the film between DeBuin and his commanding officer, Major Cartwright (Douglas Wilson).

"Do you know what General Sheridan said of this country, lieutenant?" asks the Major. "He said if he owned hell and Arizona, he'd live in hell and rent out Arizona."

"I think he said that about Texas, sir," remarks DeBuin.

"Maybe. But he *meant* Arizona."

Bruce Davison, fresh from his success in the rat revenge horror *Willard* (1971), is excellent as DeBuin, a man caught between his Christian belief and upbringing and the reality of conflict, striving and failing to understand the Apache psyche.

Mexican actor Jorge Luke brings a stillness and dignity to Ke-Ni-Tay, as does fellow countryman Joaquín Martínez as Ulzana. Luke, in particular, was sadly underused in English-language cinema, mostly playing minor villains. Martinez enjoyed greater Hollywood recognition, appearing in *Jeremiah Johnson* and *Joe Kidd* (both 1972), among others.

Richard Jaeckel features in an important supporting role as the patrol's sergeant, a man who hates and fears the Apache but, as is emblematic of the film as a whole, is far removed from the "only-good-Indian-is-a-dead-Indian" stereotype. ("Christ never fetched no infant child out of a cactus tree, then waited around for two hours so he could bury it, did he, sir? Ain't nobody gonna tell me to turn to other cheek to no Apache..."). Jaeckel, a respected character actor with an illustrious career, was an Aldrich regular, having appeared in *Attack!* (1956), *4 For Texas* (1963) and *The Dirty Dozen* (1967).

As a side note, Nick Cravat - Lancaster's partner in their circus acrobat days and later on screen in such energetic swashbucklers as *The Flame and the Arrow* (1950) and *The Crimson Pirate* (1952) - makes a practically anonymous appearance as one of the cavalry troopers.

It is Lancaster who dominates the film. Laconic, grizzled and wise, McIntosh is the moral spine of *Ulzana's Raid*. As star, he is allowed a number of Pure Lancaster Moments - in particular where, at the gallop, he (or perhaps his stunt double) throws his Winchester rifle into the air and catches it, or the heroic gravitas of his death scene. If such moments run the risk of diluting the essential realism of the film, they still serve as genuine cinematic spectacle, however brief.

Later, the detachment comes upon another plundered homestead, where the Apache have tortured the rancher to death over a slow fire, gang-raped his wife (Dran Hamilton) and left her alive. DeBuin is forced to split his command in order to send her to safety. The Apache (horseless by now thanks to McIntosh) intend to ambush the slow-moving party and take their horses, whereas DeBuin, acting on McIntosh's advice, plans to spring a counter-trap. The ensuing climax is bloody, bungled and confused, leading to a victory of sorts for the cavalry. But unlike Ford, there are no glorious charges en masse, with bugles sounding and guidons snapping proudly in the wind (although Aldrich does make satiric use of the trope by having the rescuers arrive too late to be of use). Rather, it is a montage of falling men, falling horses, the enemy all but unseen, and at one point McIntosh carrying out the mercy killing of a wounded soldier and being fatally wounded himself.

Although not a financial success upon release, the film has grown in reputation and is one of the finest westerns of the '70s (indeed, one of the finest ever made). As such, it's hard to refute the assertion of British critic Tom Milne - echoed by Edwin T. Arnold and Eugene L. Miller in their highly recommended book 'The Films and Career of Robert Aldrich' (1986) - that *Ulzana's Raid* is Aldrich's masterpiece.

POND SCUM OF THE EARTH
REMEMBERING FROGS by Steven West

"Suppose nature gave a war and everybody came: the snakes, the birds, the lizards and frogs… and suppose the polluters… the species on Earth called man were the enemy in that war - and then suppose that the human race lost…" (*Frogs* theatrical trailer)

Long before animal revolts became commonplace on our screens, British horror fiction regularly turned to Mother Nature as a force to be feared. The first 'Fontana Book of Great Horror Stories', published in 1966, contains a memorably disturbing image of a frog bloodily impaled on a darning needle. The visual accompanies Nigel Kneale's 1949 tale 'The Pond', in which an old man captures, kills and skins frogs for his own homemade diorama - and meets an inevitable, ironic, slimy demise. It's a stark precursor to *Frogs* (1972), an underrated entry in the '70s nature-on-the-rampage cycle.

American International Pictures (AIP) were a key player in the over-sized natural monster cycle of the '50s which included teen-pitched fare like *Earth vs the Spider* (1958). It's entirely fitting, then, that AIP (ever keen to sniff out a cinematic trend) dabbled with the '70s nature-strikes-back sub-genre, which was effectively the equivalent of the creature features from the A-bomb era.

Frogs, released in March 1972, emerged at a challenging time for James H. Nicholson and Samuel Z. Arkoff's independent production company. Its formula for commercial success had hitherto pivoted around an acronym of the latter's surname (yes, one "f" in Arkoff stood for "fornication").

By the time *Jaws* (1975) came along, the B-movie themes in which Arkoff and Nicholson specialised became officially intertwined with Hollywood blockbusters. AIP were already struggling to understand and fulfil the shifting expectations of post-*Easy Rider* (1969) audiences. Apart from the belated hag-horror *Whoever Slew Auntie Roo?* (1971) and occasional co-productions, the British arm of the company was extinguished. With Nicholson's departure (and subsequent death), Arkoff considered horror out of fashion and, eyeing up MGM's *Shaft* (their 3rd highest grosser of 1971), opted to embrace blaxploitation in his effort to change AIP's fortunes. The company's 1972 line-up balanced the likes of Scorsese's *Boxcar Bertha* and *Dr. Phibes Rises Again* with *Slaughter* and *Blacula*.

Frogs was almost a decade too late to be considered an opportunistic riff on *The Birds* (1963) but Hitchcock's warning of Mother Nature's apocalyptic wrath was timelier than ever and had proven influential on the wider genre, particularly George Romero's seminal containment movie *Night of the Living Dead* (1968). As we pass various 21st century environmental tipping points en route to potential oblivion, it is depressing to reflect that the early '70s brought both awareness and policy change in terms of the shifting balance between us and nature - and positive ways in which it could be stabilised.

A young Al Gore exposed political corruption for 'The Tennessean'. British meteorologist John Stanley Sawyer's 1972 study predicted an 0.6-degree global temperature rise by the end of the 20th century thanks to humanity's CO_2 overkill. Prior to this, the first nationwide Earth Day took place in 1970. President Nixon launched the Environmental Protection Agency. Greenpeace was founded in Victoria in 1971, signalling a growing movement to avoid such concerning and dangerous environmental developments. In 1974, British chemist F. Sherwood Rowland and Mexican environmental scientist Mario J. Molina published a direct warning in 'Nature' magazine about the ozone layer's depletion courtesy of aerosol spray cans. This inspired the premise and opening crawl of William Girdler's *The Day of the Animals* (1976), in which ozone deterioration results in a mass-species assault in Northern California and (more disturbingly) sleazy ad exec Leslie Nielsen hitting children and wrestling grizzly bears.

Movies capitalised on the alarm raised by the experts, though horror fiction had been exploring humankind's vulnerability in a natural crisis decades prior to Daphne Du Maurier's eerie 1952 short story 'The Birds'. Writer David Seltzer, who sounded the apocalypse-horn with the portentous *The Omen* (1976), crafted the Oscar/BAFTA-winning hybridised documentary *The Hellstrom Chronicle* (1971), incorporating clips from fictional horrors like *Them!* (1954) to reinforce the grim predictions of the fictional Dr. Nils Hellstrom (Lawrence Pressman) that Man will inevitably fall to smarter, more enduring species - specifically, insects. Like an Attenborough-sponsored precursor to *Faces of Death*, it foresees us deposed and succeeded by the creatures we already despise and fear: "The mere threat of a having an insect crawl up in your face is enough to make a man beg for mercy and tell every secret he knew."

Released four months after *Frogs* to somewhat more acclaim, *Deliverance* summarises the unease of the natural revolt horror film (and anticipates the end of 1982's *The Thing*) with a single line: "Let's just wait and see what comes out of the river." Boorman's film is as bleak in its environmental outlook as any of the era's horror movies, its protagonists seizing a chance to see the "last untamed, unpolluted, un-fucked-up river in the whole South" before it succumbs to industry and lamenting the "rape of this whole goddam landscape." Beyond the physical violence they suffer from fellow humans, the picture captures the sense of our entire system failing, the abundant litter fouling its spectacular locations representing a human signature on the contract of its imminent demise. "Christ, what a view," enthuses survivor Jon Voight, in climactic, awestruck wonder at the moonlit river after emerging from his Appalachian ordeal with presumably life-changing PTSD.

For some double feature engagements, *Frogs* was paired with another genre film with an overriding ecological message, *Godzilla vs. the Smog Monster* (1971) and, like *Deliverance*, stages its central horrors during daylight hours in areas of natural (spoiled) beauty. Mario Tosi, later cinematographer of De Palma's *Carrie* (1976), shot it around Wesley House, an old Southern mansion near the Choctawhatchee Bay on the Emerald Coast of Florida. Co writer Robert Blees - credited with Robert Hutchison

- had some form in this field, having scripted the gruesome *The Black Scorpion* (1957), alongside the *Dr. Phibes* sequel and the overlooked Tom Skerritt lion-attack shocker *Savage Harvest* (1981).

Canadian director George McCowan, whose workmanlike oeuvre includes *Shadow of the Hawk* (1976), was known for his efficiency, though reportedly resented the Grade Z material and spent much of the shoot inebriated, with assistant directors taking the reins. Producer George Edwards, in conversation with David Del Valle, relayed how veteran star Ray Milland (also one of the heads in A.I.P's bonkers *The Thing with Two Heads* that year) had a miserable experience - the intense heat melting off his toupee and contractual obligation forcing him to participate in a script he found woefully lacking in substance beyond its main concept. We might safely assume that Milland channelled this contempt into the authentic grouchiness of his (intentionally) unlikeable character - though he didn't stick around for his own death scene, having walked off the set three days earlier in disgust (it was completed using a double).

Pre-empting the pomp and festivities that would provide a populous moving-feast backdrop for *Jaws*, the picture unfolds with unsubtle irony during Milland's 4th of July celebrations. While Hitchcock was never one to hide his misanthropy and mischievously cruel streak, relishing scenes of screaming kids savaged by *The Birds*, *Frogs* and most of its stablemates offered a revolving door of odious, deservedly doomed representations of thoughtless humanity.

It begins almost by resuming where Hitch left off: the revolt is clearly underway already. The dialogue-free opening minutes echo the periods of silence/near-silence that punctuate *The Birds*, in turn foreshadowing the disturbingly quiet final half-hour of Colin Eggleston's masterful *Long Weekend* (1978). Sam Elliott (sans facial hair and reportedly source of much on-set arousal) is a handsome, heroic personification of the green movement. Researching a timely ecological magazine spread about pollution, he photographs a littered landscape akin to *Deliverance*: dead ducks surrounded by the detritus of our consumerist society (plastic dolls, Coke cans, papers) and wild woodland animals fatally impacted by poisons and pesticides. The plot catalyst, equivalent to Melanie Daniels' early encounter with a gull, has Elliott knocked out of his canoe by siblings Adam Roarke and Joan Van Ark, carelessly showing off a symbol of privilege - a trendy speedboat - and offering hospitality at their grandfather's (Milland) private island. Recurring cutaways reveal the eponymous frogs, and other species, gathering in a conspiratorial fashion, patiently watching and waiting.

Prefiguring later weather events in the U.K. (and a 1976 ladybird invasion that fed into Britain's fad for gloriously grisly eco-horror paperbacks), *Frogs* unfolds during a heatwave that Milland's self-centred family find hard to cope with. Nature, at best is an irritant: "I hate those things, they make so much noise," moans Lynn Borden as the frogs keep them all awake at night. Her materialistic discontent at the natural world would find echoes in horror films to come, from the city dwellers marooned in Wes Craven's *The Hills Have Eyes* (1977) to Ruth Roman's marvellously ironic line in *The Day of the Animals*: "I should be in Beverly Hills, where any civilised person would be!" A sense of growing unease is enhanced by one character's tabloid-like observation of the biggest bullfrog he's ever seen (the film's only nod to the oversized beasts sometimes proffered by eco horror films) while Elliott, as the voice of reason (and the ecologists), highlights the impact Milland's drastic "solutions" will have on ecosystems.

Surrounded by human-vultures with beady eyes on his fortune, Milland is a convincingly embittered, wheelchair-bound old bastard, self-aware enough to describe the assembled collective as the "ugly rich" as conversations revolve around dividends and taxes. "It's not the end of the world," he scoffs at one point, despite evidence to the contrary, and, in opposition to Hellstrom's argument, sneers at Elliott's plea for us to live in harmony with nature - considering Man the master of the world. Typical for the sub-genre, Elliott is the only one perceptive enough to realise the severity of the situation (and bold enough to admit fear). Like John Hargreaves' obnoxious, destructive *Long Weekend* protagonist, Milland seals his fate early on by killing a snake wrapped around his swish dining room chandeliers - the equivalent of a character going for a scantily clad nocturnal woodland wander at Camp Crystal Lake. And, like Murray Hamilton's Amity Mayor in the first two *Jaws* movies, he refuses to let a mounting body count intrude on his celebrations.

McCowan achieves small, effective moments of encroaching menace that nod to the remarkable jungle gym sequence in *The Birds* while echoing Hitchcock's exploitation of the subconscious intimidation birds induce in us all (eye-pecking beaks, instant humiliation of being shat on from above). Frogs (and a brief bird attack) aside, the rampaging creatures here are largely those most of us already consider repulsive: snakes, tarantulas, lizards, leeches, alligators - all of which would get further attention in the horror cinema of the '70s and '80s. Like its high-profile predecessor, the horrors unravel at a deliberate pace, with the first "attack"

at the half-way mark. It also relies on the zombie/slasher movie trope of characters foolishly wandering alone into the paths of typically slow-moving 'monsters' - though the set pieces are well handled, and the tension sustained, with the underlying hint that everybody else's 4th of July is being ruined around the U.S.

Like the irresponsible shaggers and pranksters of a *Friday the 13th* movie, much of the fun is bearing witness to deserving folks meeting unpleasant ends. A hunter is enveloped by creatures from the undergrowth after accidentally shooting himself with his own shotgun; Shaun Hutson would take this to its zenith in *Slugs* with the shmuck who blows himself up after hacking off a slug-munched hand. Lizards knock over poison jars for an amusing greenhouse fatality and frogs smugly ruin the delightful buffet spread laid out by Milland's underlings. It's shot through with a healthy sense of dark humour as

obnoxious supporting flesh-bags panic while corpses are tucked away to avoid killing the party mood.

Typical of the cycle, Milland stubbornly, sarcastically refuses to consider that Mother Nature could defeat Man to the end: "The frogs are thinking now, the snails are planning a strategy, their brains are as good as ours - is that what you're saying?" He is the 1972 horror movie equivalent of a sceptical 2022 western consumer, happy to scoff at climate change as an existential threat, unwilling to entertain the idea of their mewling McDonalds-chomping offspring facing the worst possible future. In the story's grimmest irony, the character most attuned to the natural world and our need to respect it, is forced to shoot at alligators to save innocent lives at risk- though, like everything else, it's all for nought. A marvellously hollow rescue hints at the bigger, graver picture. The final invasion of Milland's home space suggests belated pangs of guilt from all his wall-mounted animal trophies as the frogs overwhelm him.

Frogs' overall impact is heightened by Les Baxter's experimental score, sacrificing melodies and conventional horror music for a suitably alienating soundtrack to this ecological uprising. Baxter cranked out many horror scores for AIP - usually with two weeks to compose and 4-6 hours to record the music - and in 1972, worked solo on

both this and Mario Bava's *Baron Blood*. Far from resenting his genre typecasting, Baxter noted in interviews that the more horror scores he created, the more opportunities he found to experiment, *Frogs being* a distinctive example. Scored entirely with synthesised sounds, incorporating slowed-down audio of taped frogs, its unique creation prompted him, when asked by the Academy with whom he had collaborated on its atonal soundtrack, to reply: "Just me and the frogs."

The film's undeservedly mediocre reputation seems partly linked to its inclusion in Harry and Michael Medved's lame, chuckle-free 'The Golden Turkey Awards'. In his otherwise excellent AIP history 'Rock 'n' Roll Monsters', even Bruce Hallenbeck notes that *Frogs* is "often considered one of the worst horror films of all time." In reality, it's a satisfyingly sour, sometimes witty nature-amok chiller, with a post-credits image of an animated frog swallowing a human hand that suggests no one was taking it too seriously. Memorably accompanied by the tagline "Today the pond, tomorrow the world!" (and the Hitchcockian "Frogs is Coming!"), it holds up as a deliciously misanthropic addition to one of horror's bleakest and - thanks to immense ecological damage wrought by mankind in the decades since - most depressingly relevant cycles.

A.I.P., despite a major success with *The Amityville Horror* (1979), collapsed at the end of the decade, though enjoyed one of their biggest late-period hits with Bert I. Gordon's *The Food of the Gods* (1976) and *Empire of the Ants* (1977), both offering feature length critiques of humanity's polluting ways. A suitably grubby paperback successor to *Frogs* was Robin Evans' novel 'Croak', published by Hamlyn in 1981 and with the splendid tagline "From out of the marshes came a slimy, slithering nightmare" adorning a great cover image of a naked man trapped inside a giant frog's massive vocal sac. Meanwhile, in the real world, President Carter's progressive blowing of the trumpet for renewable energy at the end of the '70s would be effectively rolled back by Mr. Reagan during the 'Greed is Good' decade.

Jane Fonda in the '70s

by John H. Foote

It is impossible to measure the staggering impact of Jane Fonda. She did not just open the door for actresses in the '70s. She kicked it down and stomped on it, proving women could be every bit as realistic and brilliant as men. With her super back-to-back performances in *They Shoot Horses, Don't They?* (1969) and *Klute* (1971), she swept the year's film awards for the latter, winning many for the former. There was something unique about Fonda: she had the raw makings of a movie star - beautiful, sexy and provocative. But she was also whip-smart, fiercely opinionated and courageous.

She opposed American involvement in Vietnam and was fearless in speaking out, even when it threatened her career.

It was a single photograph that derailed the career of Fonda in the '70s, a shot of her sitting on an anti-aircraft gun belonging to the Vietcong and used to shoot down American soldiers. That shot caused a sensation in the US, and along with her anti-war sentiments, which she was in no way alone in expressing, Fonda very nearly saw the end of her film career, which had in recent years exploded.

And finally, her fitness videos sold billions through the '80s, and her fitness regime helped many men and women in their fight for good health.

Throughout it all, her film career evolved.

Today she is acting in her popular Netflix comedy *Grace and Frankie,* which attracts acclaim and an annual Emmy nomination for her and Lily Tomlin, friends since *Nine to Five.* The program has brought to the forefront the plight of senior women in the world, who they are, who they are trying to be, their sexuality and their place in society. And they are hilarious together.

Best known as a light comedic actor at the beginning of her career, she delighted audiences in the fun-filled western *Cat Ballou* (1965), which won Lee Marvin a surprise Academy Award for Best Actor, stealing the film as dead-eyed Kid Shelleen. Since her debut back in the early '60s, Fonda grew considerably as an actress, studying at Lee Strasberg's Theatre and Film Institute in New York. Her performance in Neil Simon's *Barefoot in the Park* (1967) launched her as a star on the rise. So much more than Henry's daughter and Peter's sister, she had come into her own. Then came the science fiction sex romp *Barbarella* (1968), which saw her disrobe over the opening credits, putting her spectacular body on display. Her husband Roger Vadim encouraged it, her father was appalled, her brother embarrassed, but many red-blooded American males loved it. Fonda was a sensation and on the cusp of becoming so much more.

Speaking of her father, the relationship between Henry and his daughter was never close. In fact, he kept the suicide of her mother a secret from her for years. Henry was a cold man, and while he would help her financially from time to time through her life, love or displays of affection were rare, praise, even less frequent.

Her searing performance in *They Shoot Horses, Don't They?* (1969) announced her arrival as a major new dramatic talent. As Gloria, a cynical, seething woman who has come to hate everything about life, she was sensational. Many agree it was the best performance ever by an actress. Fonda won the coveted New York Film Critics Award for Best Actress and was nominated for an Academy Award for Best Actress, one of nine nominations the film received. It also received major nominations: Best Director (Sydney Pollack), Best Supporting Actor (Gig Young), Best Supporting Actress (Susannah York), Best Screenplay Adaptation, Best Production Design, Best Costume Design, Best Film Editing and Best Musical Score. Incredibly, it was not up for Best Picture, making it the most nominated film not to receive a Best Picture nomination. Fonda was the clear leader for Best Actress but lost the award to Maggie Smith in *The Prime of Miss Jean Brodie* (1969).

Her performance in *Klute* certainly shocked the Hollywood community who had not expected Henry's little girl to match and even surpass his talent as an actor. Much was made of the nudity and sex scenes, but she defended her decision saying it was necessary for the role. And not many argued. She was scorching hot. Her character development dared to go where only men had gone. She convinced us that women could be as dark and as complex as the men in their work. Very few performances in the history of cinema have had the impact this one did for women in movies. She advanced the superb, groundbreaking work of Maria Falconetti in *The Passion of Joan of Arc* (1927), Vivien Leigh in *Gone with the Wind* (1939) and Faye Dunaway in *Bonnie and Clyde* (1967).

After working with an actor's director like Sydney Pollack, Fonda wanted someone similar for *Klute* and got just that with Alan J. Pakula. In the film, she portrays a prostitute in New York City studying to be an actress. She is a high-end prostitute, and

the wages sustain her. At one point, she realizes she is being stalked by one of her clients and is terrified. For her research, Fonda spent time with New York prostitutes, and learned a great deal. She spoke with Pakula about her time with these women and he encouraged her to use her observations to develop her role. She worked hard on her appearance, deciding on her shag haircut that would become her trademark and ubiquitous in early '70s fashion.

As Bree Daniels in *Klute*, surprisingly not the title character, she was simply a revelation, giving a performance for the ages, and one that critics began hailing as a work of art. She is beautiful and sexy yet hard and tough; this shifts to vulnerable and terrified, especially when she realizes she is being stalked. The title name, Klute, belongs to the investigator looking into a disappearance, portrayed by Donald Sutherland, coming from his starring role in *M*A*S*H* (1970). Daniels does her best

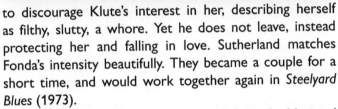

Eagle,
Veldini,
Iris,
Duval and
The Kid.

They're not
criminals...
just outlaws.

Jane **Donald**
Fonda **Sutherland**
Peter
Boyle in

Steelyard
Blues

to discourage Klute's interest in her, describing herself as filthy, slutty, a whore. Yet he does not leave, instead protecting her and falling in love. Sutherland matches Fonda's intensity beautifully. They became a couple for a short time, and would work together again in *Steelyard Blues* (1973).

Fonda swept the Best Actress awards from the National Society of Film Critics, the New York Film Critics, the National Board of Review, the Golden Globe and finally the Academy Award. By the night of the Oscars, all of Hollywood held its breath wondering what she would say for her acceptance speech, and whether she would use the platform to speak out against the Vietnam War. To their surprise, she displayed immense class, saying only: "there is a lot to say, but tonight is not the time." With her wins, she became the go-to actress, the one everyone wanted to work with.

But *Steelyard Blues* faltered at the box office and Fonda had angered the American public with her anti-war photo, labeling her 'Hanoi Jane.' Years later, she stated that she had no idea she was being positioned for a photo and would certainly not have allowed it if she did. That said, she did it, and the photo was out there. Hollywood turned

its back on this massive talent, and she went off to fight for Women's Rights, for Vietnam Veteran's Rights and to help her husband's political career.

She was away from film for several years before returning in a cameo role in the American-Russian production of *The Blue Bird* (1976) portraying Night. Looking terrific on screen, and with a solid performance, she decided it was safe to return to Hollywood.

Fonda returned to her roots in comedic roles first, doing

Fun with Dick and Jane (1977), a comedy about a couple down on their luck who begin robbing banks and stores to stay afloat. Together with George Segal, a major comedic actor in the '70, they delivered a popular, very funny film. Though hardly award worthy, it was a hit with audiences and proved Fonda was back.

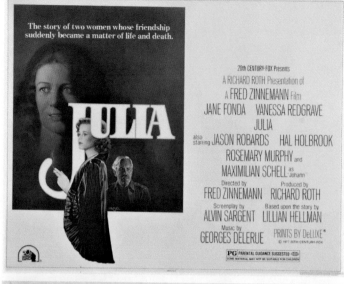

From there, she offered us great films in quick succession. *Julia* (1977), in which she portrayed writer Lillian Hellman, was directed by Fred Zinnemann, a superb film casting her

alongside Vanessa Redgrave and the great Jason Robards. It explored the friendship between Hellman and freedom fighter Julia, who fought the Nazis and left a great impact on Hellman. She would write about Julia for the rest of her life off and on, and the specter of Julia was always close, haunting her. Fonda won her second Golden Globe Award for Best Actress (Drama) and was nominated for her third Academy Award as Best Actress. It should be noted that during the shooting of *Julia*, Fonda met a rising young actress named Meryl Streep, who portrayed one of her friends in the film. Recognizing blazing talent at once, Fonda carefully guided the actress through the mechanics of filmmaking and, upon completion of the film, sang her praises. When her dear friend Alan J. Pakula was casting *Sophie's Choice* (1982) and mentioned Streep to Fonda, she told him to cast her, that no one else could do the part better. He did and Streep responded with what might be the greatest performance in film history, winning the Academy Award and every other award available to her at that time. Streep has never forgotten it and holds Jane Fonda in very high esteem.

The year 1978 would be the beginning of the most exceptional two years in Fonda's career. She would appear in three films throughout the year, one of which would

WINNER OF **3** ACADEMY AWARDS
BEST ACTRESS
Jane Fonda
BEST ACTOR
Jon Voight
BEST ORIGINAL SCREENPLAY

A JEROME HELLMAN Production
A HAL ASHBY Film

Jane Fonda
Jon Voight Bruce Dern
in
"Coming Home"

Screenplay by WALDO SALT and ROBERT C. JONES Story by NANCY DOWD
Director of Photography HASKELL WEXLER Associated Producer BRUCE GILBERT
Produced by JEROME HELLMAN Directed by HAL ASHBY   United Artists
A Transamerica Company

win her a second Academy Award, the second a powerful western directed by her friend Alan J. Pakula, and the third a box-office hit of an adaptation of a Neil Simon comedy.

She spoke out at this time that she would only be accepting roles in films she deemed important and worth her time. By turning down *An Unmarried Woman* (1978), she proved she was true to her word. Her passion project was, of course, a film about the war in Vietnam, and she commissioned a screenplay from Nancy Dowd, the creator of the salty screenplay for Paul Newman's hockey comedy *Slap Shot* (1977). Fonda knew with Dowd she would get an honest and powerful story that she could be proud of. Hal Ashby, one of the '70s great realist directors, was her choice to make the film, with two roles for actors to be filled. Her first choice for Luke Martin was Jack Nicholson, but he was everyone's first choice at the time. He declined the role and regretted it the rest of his life. Sylvester Stallone was approached until someone gathered collection of their senses, and finally Jon Voight was chosen. For the part of her husband, a hawk who succumbs to the nightmare of the war, Bruce Dern was cast.

They found that Ashby was never married to the screenplay and liked to improvise. Some of the finest moments in the film were those they created on the spot. Fonda played Sally, wife to Bob Hyde (Dern) who is shipping out to war. In one scene, we see them go through the motions of intercourse one more time before he ships out and witness an obvious lack of passion in their mechanical, boring lovemaking. While Bob is gone to war, Sally changes a great deal. She takes a volunteer job in the Veteran's Hospital and encounters Luke Martin, a guy she went to high school with. He was quarterback for the high school team, well liked by all, and now paralyzed from the waist down after an injury at war. The more time they spend together, the more they like one another. The sexual tension between them is electric, but when Bob gets liberty in Hong Kong, she dutifully goes. He is not happy she is working, not at all, and angered that part of her work is massaging the vets. But Bob is having his own troubles, struggling with the war and what his men are doing.

"My men were chopping off heads, because that was what they into," he tells her before crashing on the bed to sleep with a loaded weapon.

Sally comes home to find Luke involved in the anti-war movement after a young man they both know kills himself. She goes to Luke's place with him and experiences her first orgasm. With Luke, she finds her world opens up and she discovers things about herself she had not previously known. When Bob returns, he is in no way prepared for what he discovers about his wife. It starts right at the airport where he comments about her hair, followed by a comment about their car, then the beach house ("You're full of surprises!") before heading out to be with a bunch of veterans also returning home. Told by the military about her affair with Luke, Bob's world spirals out of control and he threatens both Luke and Sally with a loaded rifle, before realizing what he is doing. He has returned home under mysterious circumstances (is his wound self-inflicted?) and with a medal. The look on his face tells us he is ashamed of having the medal pinned on him, he did nothing heroic to deserve it, but he goes through with the charade.

The movie ends with Bob heading to the sandy beach. There, ceremoniously, he takes off his uniform, gently, with care, until he is entirely naked and then heads out to sea, to his death. Defeated by the war, by himself and in a sense, by the betrayal of his wife, Bob is finished.

Released in springtime, *Coming Home* received excellent reviews and decent but not great box office. Voight and Dern earned the better reviews, but Fonda received her share of accolades too. She had long ago conceded the film was about the men who fought the war. Re-released in December of the same year, after Jon Voight began winning Best Actor awards for his work, the film was nominated for eight Academy Awards. Its chief competition was *The Deer Hunter* (1978), another film about Vietnam but, we would learn, predicated on the lies of its director/co-writer Michael Cimino. On Oscar night, *Coming Home* won three Academy Awards: Best Actor for Voight, Best Original Screenplay and for Fonda,

Alan Alda   **Walter Matthau**
Michael Caine   **Elaine May**
Bill Cosby   **Richard Pryor**
Jane Fonda   **Maggie Smith**

NEIL SIMON'S
CALIFORNIA SUITE

The best two-hour vacation in town!

COLUMBIA PICTURES PRESENTS A RAY STARK PRODUCTION · A HERBERT ROSS FILM
NEIL SIMON'S CALIFORNIA SUITE
starring ALAN ALDA · MICHAEL CAINE · BILL COSBY · JANE FONDA
WALTER MATTHAU · ELAINE MAY · RICHARD PRYOR · MAGGIE SMITH
Screenplay by NEIL SIMON · Produced by RAY STARK · Directed by HERBERT ROSS

her second Oscar as Best Actress. Dern was robbed as was director Hal Ashby for what was his finest film and remains one of the greatest films about the plight of the Vietnam veteran. Fonda was satisfied, she had finally made a film that spoke to the nation about the veterans. She had used her art for the greater good.

California Suite was a hit (most Neil Simon adaptations were) but it is not remembered as one of his greatest films or, for that matter, Fonda's. It is an ensemble piece set in a California hotel about a group of couples dealing with various aspects of their marriage. Fonda was paired with

Alan Alda as a bickering couple at war over the custody of their child. It was the least comedic of the stories, and though well- acted, unmemorable.

Her third film of 1978 was a modern-day western *Comes a Horseman*, beautifully photographed, and very well acted, especially by supporting actor Richard Farnsworth and Fonda, but the film dragged, and James Caan struck no sparks with her. He looked the part as the modern cowboy, but there was nothing believable between the two of them.

The following year she gave a superb performance in *The China Syndrome* (1979) as a TV reporter who stumbles onto a story about the cover-up of a radioactive leak at a nuclear plant. As Kimberly, she settles into the role of the ambitious but never sleazy news reporter who just wants the truth. She and her cameraman, portrayed by a young Michael Douglas, witness the accident, he shoots it, and they know they have a story. However, the foreman at the plant, played brilliantly by Jack Lemmon, will not talk about the accident until he realizes his superiors are trying to cover up the event. At that point he knows he must talk, despite what they think, despite the damage that could come to the plant. He lets us know just how close the plant came to a nuclear disaster, always a threat when using nuclear power.

The film received the best free publicity possible when a real-life accident happened at Three Mile Island within days of the film's opening. Suddenly cinema was life, and it was terrifying. Audiences flocked to see it, and critics raved about the performances of Lemmon and Fonda, their superb work landing them both Oscar nominations in leading roles. The manner in which the plant cover-up took place, and the involvement of the government, frightened the public, leading to demands for greater transparency about the risks of nuclear power.

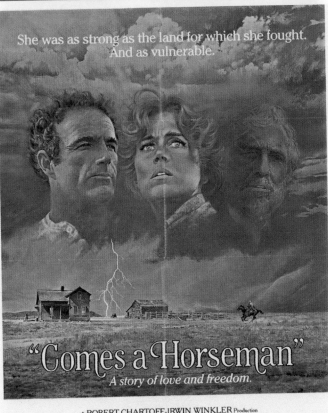

She was as strong as the land for which she fought. And as vulnerable.

"Comes a Horseman"
A story of love and freedom.

A ROBERT CHARTOFF-IRWIN WINKLER Production
An ALAN J. PAKULA Film
JAMES CAAN JANE FONDA JASON ROBARDS
"COMES A HORSEMAN"
Music by MICHAEL SMALL Director of Photography GORDON C. WILLIS, A.S.C.
Written by DENNIS LYNTON CLARK Produced by GENE KIRKWOOD and DAN PAULSON
Executive Producers IRWIN WINKLER and ROBERT CHARTOFF Directed by ALAN J. PAKULA
United Artists

People who know the meaning of "The China Syndrome" are scared...
...soon you will know.

JACK LEMMON   JANE FONDA   MICHAEL DOUGLAS

the China Syndrome

COLUMBIA PICTURES PRESENTS A MICHAEL DOUGLAS/IPC FILMS PRODUCTION A JAMES BRIDGES FILM
JACK LEMMON   JANE FONDA   MICHAEL DOUGLAS
THE CHINA SYNDROME
Written by MIKE GRAY & T.S. COOK and JAMES BRIDGES · Associate Producer JAMES NELSON
Executive Producer BRUCE GILBERT · Produced by MICHAEL DOUGLAS · Directed by JAMES BRIDGES
"Somewhere In Between" by STEPHEN BISHOP
©1979 COLUMBIA PICTURES INDUSTRIES INC

by-numbers story, enormously enjoyable to watch. I have never seen the film since first released in 1979 and have no inclination to watch it again. I know it, I can predict the narrative before it happens, it is a pure mainstream popcorn film. Perhaps it is most notable for being the film debut of singer Willie Nelson who proved to be a very fine actor.

Fonda was nominated for a third Academy Award for Best Actress for *The China Syndrome*, alongside co-star Jack Lemmon who was enjoying a career renaissance of his own. This time she lost to Sally Field in *Norma Rae* (1979), another role Fonda had passed on.

As the '70s ended, Fonda began to be recognized as a mature, intelligent actress who could stand on her own and did not need a man to define her, who could open and sell films on her own, and was among the top box office stars of the decade. More importantly, audiences looked forward to her films, women looked up to her and men admired her - she had become a role model.

No other actress had the impact on film that Jane Fonda did in the '70s. She knocked down doors, opened borders, made it possible for women to be as realistic as men on screen, and proved time and again that a woman could indeed carry a film.

Fonda is superb as Kimberly, the hard-edged news woman who finds herself mired in a deeply human story. She sees the foreman Lemmon taking the fall for the accident despite the fact he prevented it from becoming catastrophic. When the plant's administration has him killed just as another accident hits, she knows every word he has spoken was the truth. The final moments of the film are both frightening and shocking in their realism as we grow to understand just how far the company will go to protect their precious plant. Veteran Lemmon is sensational as the haggard and frightened foreman, trying to hold onto his sanity with the knowledge that something is deeply wrong.

Her other release in 1979 was a frolic more than anything else. *The Electric Horseman* partnered her with her *Barefoot in the Park* co-star Robert Redford and director Sydney Pollack. Of all the films she made in the '70s, this would be the weakest. A love story (obviously), she portrays a news woman (again) assigned a story about a former cowboy who kidnaps a horse that he believes is being abused by a company that has been using the animal for marketing. His plan is to ride the horse into the desert and set it free. Along the way, they fall in love. It is a paint-

Tell me Norman..... did you think it was going to be this tough to get rid of a pain in the ass like me?

Ma'am, I had no idea.

UNIVERSAL PICTURES and COLUMBIA PICTURES present
A RAY STARK – WILDWOOD PRODUCTION
ROBERT REDFORD
JANE FONDA
in A SYDNEY POLLACK FILM
THE ELECTRIC HORSEMAN
co-starring VALERIE PERRINE
and WILLIE NELSON
Director of Photography OWEN ROIZMAN A.S.C. Music by DAVE GRUSIN
Screenplay by ROBERT GARLAND Screen Story by PAUL GAER and ROBERT GARLAND
Produced by RAY STARK ORIGINAL SOUND TRACK ALBUM ON CBS RECORDS AND TAPES
Directed by SYDNEY POLLACK PANAVISION ® TECHNICOLOR ®
Distributed by CINEMA INTERNATIONAL CORPORATION
©1979 Universal City Studios Inc. -Columbia Pictures Industries Inc. All Rights Reserved

Tam Lin

by Simon J. Ballard

Mention the term 'folk horror', and invariably one or all of the unholy trinity - *Witchfinder General* (1968), *Blood on Satan's Claw* (1971) and *The Wicker Man* (1973) - will spring to mind. The folk horror label was popularised by Mark Gatiss for the 2010 documentary *A History of Horrors*. More recent examples of the form might include *A Field in England* (2013) and *Midsommar* (2019).

Tam Lin (1970), Roddy McDowall's only directorial feature, tends to be neglected in this arena. And that's a shame, for it is terrific - an outstanding entry in the field of folk horror. Its origins lie within a Scottish myth dating back to the 16th century, which adds weight to its folk horror label. It received a limited release in the UK in 1970, and was re-edited two years later and released in the United States under the title *The Devil's Widow*. Given this chequered release history, its neglect is easy to understand.

The movie neatly straddles the bridge between the end of one epoch and the beginning of another. Fable mixes with film, as the here-and-now of the early '70s peels back to a period of counter-cultural revolution. It may be set in contemporary times, but it harks to a period long gone, preserved through the amber of time and song, spoken and written word. Speaking of the latter, during the course of my write-up I will use italicised interjections from 'The Ballad of Tam Lin' composed by Robert Burns between 1771-79.

In essence, Burns' ballad concerns Tam Lin, a sort of elf or fairy, whose task is to collect either a possession from, or the virginity of, any maiden who passes through the forest of Carterhaugh. When one such maiden, known as Janet, plucks a double rose while travelling through the forest, Tam appears to challenge her about taking what is his. However, the two are instantly attracted and soon feel a spark of love between them. It isn't long before

Janet becomes pregnant. Tam, however, is controlled by the Queen of the Fairies. Every seven years, the Queen gives one of her people as a tithe (a sacrificial gift) to Hell, and Tam has a horrible feeling it's his turn to be the tithe this coming Hallowe'en. He tries to flee on a white horse, pursued by eleven knights, and begs Janet to rescue him by pulling him off the horse without dropping him. He warns her that the Queen may try to trick her into letting go by transforming him into a variety of beasts, but no matter what she sees she must stay firm and cling to him. Only when he turns into a lump of burning coal can she finally drop him, by throwing him into a well. If she does this, he will become human once more. This will anger the Queen, but she will nevertheless be forced to acknowledge defeat and set Tam free for good.

American writer/producer/director William Spier was tasked with transforming this folk tale into a 20th century film interpretation. A very fine cast was assembled to breathe life into the myth. Foremost was Ava Gardner, tempted out of semi-retirement by McDowall to play the mysterious and immensely wealthy Michaela Cazaret (the film's Queen of the Fairies figure). In the ballad tradition of lowland Scotland, the Queen was often named Elphane which, in turn, has been associated with the name Morgan (as in Morgan le Fay, of Arthurian legend). Morgan le Fay = Michaela Cazaret in the screen version (the two names sound loosely similar if you say them aloud). Michaela fears that age will wither her infinite variety, so she assembles an entourage of not-so-bright (but beautiful) young things to be her loyal minions. These include the likes of Madeline Smith, Joanna Lumley and Bruce Robinson (the latter of whom, incidentally, would go on to direct the cult favourite *Withnail & I!*)

Totally and utterly devoted to Michaela (or Micky, as she's affectionately called) is Tom Lynn, a young handsome man whom she has taken as her lover. Ian McShane, with his youthful, chiselled looks and beguiling green eyes, is cast as Tom. He portrays him as a shell of a man who cannot perform away from the enchantments of Micky's allure. All that changes when he meets Janet Ainsley (Stephanie Beacham). Beacham, very early into her film career, is stunningly assured as Janet, running the gamut of emotions through her facial expression alone, which is no mean feat.

The initial meeting between Tam and Janet takes place within the grounds of Micky's fairy castle-like house in the lush, green surrounds of Carter Hall. In dowdy brown attire, Janet enters what seems to be a hippy commune.

"Four and twenty bodies fair,
We playing at the ba,
And out then cam fair Janet Ance,
The flower among them a'."

Fairy-tale imagery is mingled with the end of the '60s dream, with the gathered crowd representing the hopes and idealisations of a movement that was rapidly assaulted by the death of innocence in the face of the ongoing war in Vietnam and the Manson killings. (Eerily, I made that connection shortly before listening to an audio interview with McShane, in which recalled hearing about the murder of Sharon Tate while filming interiors for this very film at Pinewood Studios. Creepy coincidence, or what?)

As the '70s beckoned, a new, harsh reality dug in its heels. The future was forgotten, and self-reflection or self-destruction became the order of the day. A new-found love for ancient religion vied for attention with psychotropic acid trips. *Tam Lin* came right at the apex of this dark new world. Micky may well be the Queen of the Fairies, but with the waifs and strays escaping the new decade under her protective wing, she's like the female equivalent of Ken Kesey. Her followers are like Kesey's busload of dropouts, as recorded in Tom Woolfe's 1968 account 'The Electric Kool-Aid Acid Test'. Micky *is* life, in the sense that she provides life as much as she takes it like a perpetually self-absorbing sponge.

"She had na pu'd a double rose,
A rose but only tway,
Till up then started young Tom-lin."

Bringing the gift of a puppy to the child-like, spaced-out Sue (Madeline Smith), Janet interrupts a game of catch involving Tom and two red frisbees. Their eyes meet and there is an instant connection, an attraction that at the same time strikes fear in them, a mutual wariness of the unknown. The sensation is palpable, conveyed to us as potently as if we're right there with them.

When Janet first sees Michaela, she feels briefly entranced, as though a spell has come over her. Living a humble existence in a vicarage with her vicar father (nicely underplayed by Cyril Cusack), Janet's wide-eyed appreciation of the opulent surroundings are portrayed well by Beacham. One is reminded of Gretel (of 'Hansel and Gretel') staring in amazement at the house built of layered sweetness. She projects a sense of unease as well as amazement, unsettled by the very alien land she has traversed, her gait awkward and unsure.

Janet and Tom meet on either side of a babbling brook and, as Janet feels the attraction grow, Tom takes a swig from a bottle and smashes it. We wonder if there is danger in crossing the great divide? A montage of stills follows, like something from the pages of a fairy-tale book. Janet is repulsed, nervous, and magnetically pulled at the same time. When they finally sit together, the music changes from other-worldly folk strains to something dreamier with a romantic lilt. Folk band Pentacle provide their very own Ballad of Tom Lynn. Like Burns' poem, it seeds the narrative throughout.

It is a great shame McDowall never directed another picture. He cleverly mixes the lush, natural surrounds of Scotland with the more urbanised elements seen both in the prologue and later scenes around the Forth Bridge. The suggestion is that under Micky nature has its own dangers lurking away from the rat race. McDowall excels in bringing out the depths of character in this heightened reality. The liminal lines between legendary and present times are left to the viewer's own perceptions.

Gardner is exemplary in her portrayal of the domineering yet fragile Michaela, bemoaning the fact that she is immensely old. She is utterly bereft when the formerly obsessed Tom seeks an escape with Janet. Without him, the superficialities of her groupies are highlighted. "You torpid collection," she utters at one point with barbed contempt. The groupies are mainly preoccupied with their games and chemical recreations - "I'll take anything as long as it's illegal!" Sue enthuses - and there is an air that they're marking time, keeping the next second at bay. Michaela's main fear is the withering that goes with growing old and the approaching loneliness. There may be something parasitic in her needs, but the love she feels is undeniably genuine.

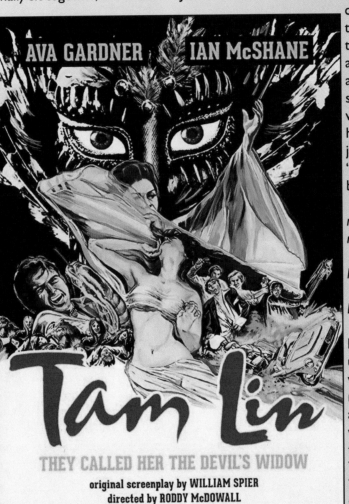

AVA GARDNER · IAN McSHANE

Tam Lin

THEY CALLED HER THE DEVIL'S WIDOW

original screenplay by WILLIAM SPIER
directed by RODDY McDOWALL

"Ay at the end of seven years,
They pay a tiend to Hell."

Michaela's confidential private secretary Elroy (a splendid Richard Wattis) warns Tom against leaving Micky. He recounts the fates of two young men who died seven years apart in road accidents, the last occurring in 1962. Elroy may be a "rancid old queen" to Tom, but an air of menace surrounds his watchful glare.

Music plays a key role throughout alongside Burns' ballad. Along with Pentacle's atmospheric narrative melody, there is the opening titles song - Sun in My Eyes sung by Salena Jones - which contains foreshadowing lyrics like: "Take care, their games could take the best part of you... let the Queen bee show you all that's you." As Micky and Tom share a stilted last supper before he is granted a week's truce to decide where his destiny lies, a singer in a jazz bar melancholically sings: "You think your love is gold, but it's turned to lead."

"Just at the murk and midnight hour the fairie will ride,
And they that wad their true love win,
At Miles Cross they maun bide."

The horror elements lurking within Tam Lin unveil their sinister head when Micky gains a new, more dangerous coven of associates. They kidnap Tom, wresting him away from his true love, the pregnant Janet. The build up of tension as Tom is forced to drink from a chalice containing some powerful hallucinogen is edgy, at times almost uncomfortable to watch. We realise Micky is making good her earlier promise to hunt him down and kill him. You might think that's a rather outré reaction for a spurned lover. In normal circumstances you'd be right, but these are far from normal circumstances.

"But quickly run to the milk-white steed and ay the nearest town."

The drugged condition of Tom makes everything that happens next subjective, very much open to interpretation. What really happens during the hunt? Micky's baying followers hotly pursue Tom in his commandeered white Aston Martin, but what are we to make of what takes place as they chase him into the woods?

"*They'll turn me to a bear sae grim.*"

Are Tom's slow-motion, agonised visions of himself wading through the nightmarish woodland and marshland, his body transformed into that of a bear, real? A spell cast by Micky in her jealous rage, perhaps? Is he merely undergoing the trip from Hell? You could legitimately accept any of those interpretations.

"*They'll turn me in your arms, lady, into…an adder…*
And last they'll turn me, in your arms, into the burning lead;
Then throw me into the well-water,
O throw me in wi' speed!"

As for the closing moments of the ballad as set down by Robert Burns, there will be no spoilers here. I will leave you to discover how closely to the myth/ballad this screen version of *Tam Lin* adheres.

It is easy to see why the movie suffered poor distribution. It doesn't give answers freely and doesn't have the sort of linear narrative audiences (and financers) had come to expect from British horror at this stage in its history. Hammer, Tigon, Amicus, et al dominated the box office with more straightforward fare.

Appropriately for a film concerning an ancient legend yet steeped in the zeitgeist of the time, *Tam Lin*'s narrative and direction are simultaneously behind and ahead of their time in equal measure. Anyone who watches the film will find it lingering long in their memory. It may even encourage them to further explore retellings of the myth, ranging from Victorian fairy tale books to songs by such bands as Fairport Convention. Interestingly, Paddy Tunney (born in Glasgow to Irish parents) sang a version of *Tam Lin* in 1968, at a time when folk music was undergoing something of a revival. Ancient traditions are passed on orally, and the legend of Tam Lin has truly seeded itself through the ages. Put simply, it is folk horror at its best.

Hustle

by Dr. Andrew C. Webber

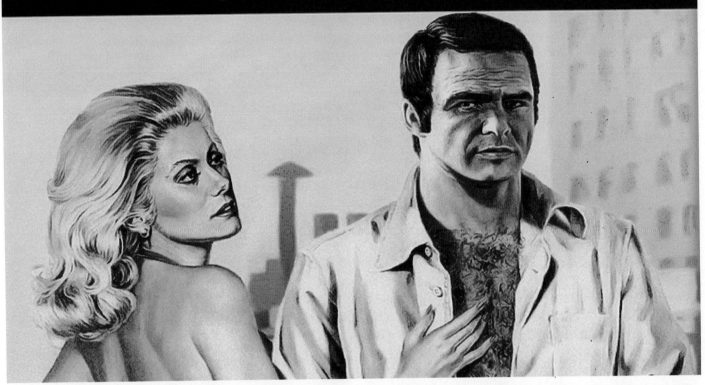

Lovers of '70s movie will know that director Robert Aldrich could boast a number of classic titles on his filmography. The anti-war movie *The Dirty Dozen* (1967) was possibly his biggest commercial success, but he also hit paydirt (and cultdom) with the brilliant noir *Kiss Me Deadly* (1955), as well as refereeing Bette Davis and Joan Crawford in their feuding roles in the now camp classic *What Ever Happened to Baby Jane?* (1962). These and other early Aldrich offerings - *Apache* and *Vera Cruz* (both 1954), *The Big Knife* (1955), *Attack!* (1956), *The Flight of the Phoenix* (1965), and *Too Late the Hero* (1970) - are easily available on DVD. His misfiring *Bonnie and Clyde* rip-off *The Grissom Gang* (1971); the still heavily cut western *Ulzana's Raid* (1972); and the smash-hit sports comedy *The Longest Yard* (aka *The Mean Machine*) (1974) are also readily available too. You can even get hold, finally, of his

thriller *Twilight's Last Gleaming* (1977) on a dual format Blu Ray disc, should you be so inclined.

That other great Robert of the era - Robert Altman - made films about communities and the messiness of living. They reminded us how we might have once lived, pre-Covid, and how much being in isolation seems to be in direct contradiction to our need to socialise. The films from Aldrich's latter career are, like Altman's from that period, far less easy to track down. Elusive Aldrich titles include his 1979 black comedy *The Choirboys* (based on a bestseller by Joseph Wambaugh, a writer of brilliant cop novels but badly served by the current unavailability of filmic adaptations of his books on home media); the oddball Gene Wilder/Harrison Ford comedy-western *The Frisco Kid* (1979); and his final film, the female wrestling drama (much better than it sounds) *All the Marbles* (aka

The California Dolls) (1981) starring Peter Falk.

This article, however, will focus on Aldrich's gloomy cop drama *Hustle* from 1975 (not to be confused with Robert Rossen's brilliant pool hall drama *The Hustler;* Jennifer Lopez's lap-dancing drama *Hustlers,* or that dreadful *Dirty Rotten Scoundrels* remake *The Hustle*). This *Hustle* stars Burt Reynolds and French beauty Catherine Deneuve (best known to audiences back then for the international success of Buñuel's *Belle de Jour*), in one of her rare forays into '70s American cinema (see also Dick Richards' Foreign Legion drama *March or Die* from 1977). *Hustle* is currently only available as an import but definitely deserves to be better known, especially by readers of this magazine who like nothing better than grubbing round in the nether corners of the era in search of elusive 'lost classics'.

Reynolds (who enjoyed his finest hour in John Boorman's *Deliverance* [1972], though the self-directed *Sharky's Machine* [1981] is also well worth a look) was a huge '70s star and sex symbol. However, he was virtually eradicated from serious film debate as the years wore on. Poor career choices saw him drop off the radar with critics and audiences alike, though his star was briefly reignited by Paul Thomas Anderson in *Boogie Nights* (1997). He died in 2018, never quite fully capitalising upon this return to the limelight.

In *Hustle* Reynolds plays against type as Phil Gaines, a cynical down-at-heel cop who's fallen in love with Deneuve's call girl Nicole Britton (this type of female character crops up a lot in '70s cinema - see *California Split* and *The Gauntlet* for further examples). They plan to leave America and live life to the full in Europe, but first Gaines must solve the death of a girl whose body has turned up on a beach. And it's one of those cases so typical of the neo-noir genre which sees him uncovering more secrets, guilt and corruption the further he delves. Steve Shagan wrote the script (he'd been nominated for an Academy Award for his debut - the Jack Lemmon pic *Save The Tiger* in 1974, which had won Lemmon his second Best Actor Oscar against stiff competition, including Nicholson, Redford and Pacino). *Hustle* also provides small roles for several character actors - Ben Johnson as a rather unsympathetic grieving father, Eddie Albert (who had played the prison warden in the previous Aldrich/Reynolds pairing *The Longest Yard*) as a smarmy but smiling businessman, and Ernest Borgnine (who had worked with Aldrich on *The Flight of the Phoenix, The Dirty Dozen, The Legend of Lylah Clare* and *Emperor of the North*) as Reynolds' gruff boss (another stereotypical character who was accepted by viewers as standard during the period).

Leslie Halliwell, whose annual guides remain indispensable for film fans even in the Digital Age, noted that *Hustle* was a "doleful crime melodrama with both eyes in the gutter", which probably explains why it's stood the test of time', unlike Reynolds' more comical vehicles

84

from the decade, like *Shamus* (1973), *Gator* (1976) and, of course, the dreadful *Smokey and the Bandit* (1977-1983) series, where his endless mugging finally got in the way of his performances.

Like Polanski's better-known *Chinatown* (1974), *Hustle* is a dark and depressing little movie in which everyone is scarred by the world's corruption and decay. And, typical of so many of the key movies of the '70s, it ends bleakly too. A bit like life, then.

Hustle is the kind of movie you can imagine being a big influence on crime novelist James Ellroy - it's surprisingly frank, grim and in its own way rather tragic, and there are certainly echoes of *The Black Dahlia* to be found amongst its thematic concerns.

Compared to Altman's movies (which are subtle, painterly and elliptical), Aldrich's films tend to provide quite a lot of bang for your buck and are renowned for their hard-hitting violence and sometimes unsubtle black humour. Neither of these qualities are particularly evident in *Hustle,* which is a melancholic film about losers, the lure of money and lost opportunities. Apparently, Reynolds wasn't happy with the finished movie and he and Aldrich parted company.

Along with Arthur Penn's 1975 noir *Night Moves*, *Hustle* is the kind of thriller that no-one is making any longer (more's the pity) and definitely a film which will make you want to have a shower after watching, should you ever come across it.

I'll be in my usual seat in NFT1 if and when an Aldrich season shows up. Let's hope it does, and let's hope *Hustle* is on the bill.

"I never miss a Liv Ullman Musical"

LOST HORIZON

by Peter Sawford

Growing up in the late '60s and early '70s, trips to the cinema were an occasional treat rather than a regular occurrence. Because of this, I can clearly remember the title of every film I went to see. But in 1973, we went to watch the musical remake of *Lost Horizon* and I remember nothing about viewing it at that time. I *can* remember that I argued strongly, as any 8-year-old would, to see Roger Moore in his debut as James Bond in *Live and Let Die* instead. But my memories of *Lost Horizon*, the film? Not a thing.

Fortunately, Talking Pictures (UK) showed it one Saturday morning a few years ago and, armed with a cup of tea and a slice of toast, I settled down to see why I didn't recall it in any way. 2½ hours late, I had my answer.

The film was the creation of producer Ross Hunter. During his time as a producer at Universal, he was responsible for a string of hits including *Magnificent Obsession* (1954), *All That Heaven Allows* (1955) and *Airport* (1970). The latter would be one of his most successful but also his last at Universal. Thereafter, he accepted an offer from Columbia to run his own production team. Wishing to make a fast start for his new bosses, Hunter looked through old Columbia properties to see if there was anything he could get to work on almost immediately and reasonably cheaply. Quickly, his eyes lit upon *Lost Horizon*.

Written by James Hilton in 1933, it told the story of a disparate group escaping from revolutionary India. En route to safety, their plane is hijacked and eventually crashes in the Himalayas. Rescued by a group of monks,

the party are taken to Shangri-La, a tropical oasis in the mountains where peace and harmony reign and people live to healthy old age.

Columbia boss Harry Cohn had snapped it up in the '30s and Frank Capra directed a highly regarded version starring Ronald Colman. Capra went so over budget and over schedule that the film took years to finally make a profit. Hunter was undaunted by this. Nor was he concerned by the failure of the 1956 Broadway musical *Shangri-La* (which had folded after just 21 performances), or the fact that the last producer to believe going through a studio's back catalogue was a cheap and cheerful solution had nearly bankrupted 20th Century Fox. He preferred instead to concentrate on the success of the 1969 remake of James Hilton's other book, 'Goodbye, Mr Chips'. Starring Petula Clark and an Oscar-nominated Peter O'Toole, the film, while not quite a resounding hit, had been well received by the critics and the public alike. Moreover, it was a musical. In Hunter's mind, if it had worked for an adaptation one of Hilton's books, it could work for the other. It was in that very moment that the decision was made to present this *Lost Horizon* as a musical.

Working on a budget close to $12m, Hunter decided only the best was good enough for his project and quickly made a list of all the things he needed to make it a success. As the decision had been made to venture down the musical route, Hunter wasted no time in signing up song writing superstars Burt Bacharach and Hal David for the score, and legendary choreographer Hermes Pan for the dance routines. Joining forces in 1957, Bacharach and David had struck gold over the next fifteen years with songs like *I Say a Little Prayer*, *Walk on By* and *The Look of Love*, while winning an Oscar for *Raindrops Keep Fallin' on my Head* in 1969. Hermes Pan had started dancing professionally as a chorus boy in 1928, but in 1933 had met Fred Astaire on the set of *Flying Down to Rio* and the two had begun a partnership on films such as *Top Hat* (1935), *Swing Time* (1936) and *The Story of Vernon and Irene Castle* (1939). Scripting duties were handed to Larry Kramer. He wasn't exactly one of the most prolific screenwriters (*Lost Horizon* would only be his third screenplay), but an Oscar nomination for *Women in Love* (1969) had certainly made him one of the most in-demand. Robert Surtees, a three-time Academy Award winner, was brought in as cinematographer. Once British director Charles Jarrott had signed on to helm, Hunter turned his attention to the cast.

British-born, Australian-raised Peter Finch, much in demand after his BAFTA-winning role in John Schlesinger's *Sunday, Bloody Sunday* (1971), was signed on to play Richard Conway, the unofficial leader of the group who struggles to decide whether to stay in this new paradise or return to the real world, while Michael York, fresh from his success in *Cabaret* (1972), was picked to play his younger brother George. Sam Cornelius, an engineer running away from a failed business and the ruin of bankruptcy, was perfect for George Kennedy. Sally Kellerman, still riding high on the crest of the wave of her triumph as Major 'Hot Lips' Houlihan in Robert Altman's *M*A*S*H* (1970) plays Sally Hughes, a neurotic, pill-popping photographer

looking for peace and a new purpose in life. Bobby Van rounded out the group by virtually playing a shadow of himself as Harry Lovett a failing song-and-dance man with a nice line in corny comedy. Of those already enjoying the long and tranquil life at Shangri-La, Charles Boyer, star of such Hollywood classics as *Algiers* (1936) and *Gaslight* (1944), is almost unrecognisable as the aged High Lama. British star of stage and screen John Gielgud was talked into playing the High Lama's loyal and faithful servant Chang, and James Shigeta (who'd been absent from the big screen since 1968's *Manila, Open City*) is Brother To-Len, the third in command. Olivia Hussey, whose career had stalled somewhat after her breakout role in *Romeo and Juliet* (1968), was cast as Maria, whose longing to leave and see the outside world leads to tragedy. But the biggest coup was convincing Norwegian superstar Liv Ullmann to take on the part of Catherine, the schoolteacher who wins the heart of Richard. Ullman, the muse of legendary director Ingmar Bergman, had starred in five of his films up to that point and *Lost Horizon* would be her debut in an American picture.

Lost Horizon was filmed between April and June 1972, with its New York premiere taking place on 14th March 1973 and it's Los Angeles premiere three days later. Such was the buzz around the film that California governor and future US president Ronald Reagan was persuaded to attend the Hollywood premiere. In Britain, it was selected for that year's Royal Film Performance The buzz lasted right up until the end credits rolled across the screen at which point the critics rushed to their typewriters and proceeded to tear the film to pieces.

The initial problem is that for a musical, the first song isn't heard until the 41st minute and the last occurs long before the end of the film. By the time the first song appears, you've got used to the film being a straight drama and are just beginning to get nicely involved in the plot when that first number breaks the rhythm. By the time Bobby Van sings *Question Me an Answer* well into the movie, you're finally in the right frame of mind to see it as a musical. But the songs stop abruptly thereafter, and for the last 40 minutes it reverts to being a non-musical drama. This has the effect of making the film feel like it was turned into a musical halfway through, that the songs were shoehorned into the middle part of the story and then the makers changed their minds back again.

The second problem was that although Bacharach and David were hugely successful, the songs they wrote were gentle and relaxed easy listening tunes. In musicals, such laidback songs don't really work. The situation wasn't helped by Hal David turning in some of his weakest, most uninspired and asinine work. *The World is a Circle* is the song you'll remember the most, but that's for Bacharach's tune rather than David's somewhat forgettable lyrics. In truth, the songs weren't helped by the dance routines worked out by Hermes Pan. Some believe that, at 63, Pan was too old and too out of touch with modern audiences, but I believe that faced with a cast that had about as much natural rhythm as a paving slab, Pan simply gave them the dance moves he believed they could handle. Therefore, we get an overabundance of arm twirls, shoulder shrugs, hip sways and the kind of soft shoe shuffles you dread your least favourite uncle performing at your wedding reception. Although it's very easy to lay all the blame at the feet of the score and dance routines, Jerry Kramer's script has to shoulder some of the blame. Being made in 1973, when the Vietnam war was coming to a close, Kramer was clearly making a point about love and understanding over hate and fighting, but it's incredibly heavy-handed and subtlety is nowhere to be found. Up to the point they arrive in Shangri-La, the characters are relatively engaging and interesting. In the early scenes, you actually care whether they'll escape from their troubled surroundings, find an aircraft that can fly them to safety and reach home. Once in paradise, the changes to their personalities arrive at bullet speed. Kramer would admit himself years later that he wasn't proud of his work on the film, but his fee would allow him to pick and choose the work he did, or didn't do, for the rest of his life.

The production wasn't helped with penny pinching when it came to set design either. The castle from 1967's *Camelot* was badly re-purposed and the rest of the set was, according to Michael York, ludicrously tacky and poor. The plane crashing into the mountains looks like an Airfix model being dropped onto a papier mâché mock-up of the mountain range. In fairness, both Robert

Surtees and Charles Jarrott do the best they can with the material they've been lumped with. The early scenes at the airstrip are suitably frantic and desperate as the group make a last-minute bid for a place on one of last few planes that can carry them to safety, away from their war-torn surroundings. Both manage to convey the panic and fear of those trapped at the airport as the sound of gunfire quickly gets closer and the number of planes just as quickly diminishes. Likewise, at the end when Richard and George are making their bid to return to the world, Surtees beautifully captures the spectacular views across the snow-covered peaks of the Himalayas (in reality the Cascade Mountains in Washington).

By and large, the cast managed to escape the debacle with their dignity and careers intact. John Gielgud regretted taking a role in the film and complained that the only acting required was the ability to walk and talk at the same time, but he obviously didn't learn much from his experience if his later role in *Caligula* was anything to go by. Peter Finch admitted that, although the finished product wasn't a thing of beauty, he did have fun making it. Finch plays Richard as a world-weary trouble-shooter, tired of trying to find answers to other people's endless questions while struggling to figure out what forces have been at play for him and the others to end up in what appears to be paradise, but potentially holds a much darker secret. Along with Peter O'Toole and Richard Harris, Finch had been one of the great hellraisers of the '50s and '60s, but while O'Toole and Harris had survived relatively intact, it had left Finch looking weather-beaten and old before his time. Although this fits in well with a character who is torn between his new life and love for Catherine and his

loyalty to his brother (who desires to return to the outside world), it would also lead to his untimely death just three years later. Sadly for Michael York he was handed just the weakest of the roles and wasn't able to do much with a cardboard cut-out of a character. George is a somewhat peripheral, one-dimensional character who makes no bones about wanting to go back to the real world, but what could have been an interesting contrast to the more accepting members of the group, he's reduced to simply walking into scenes, stating his objections to being there and walking out again.

Sam Cornelius starts off as the most interesting and well-rounded of the party, a man with a dubious and chequered past. Those who keep asking about his past are likely to end up with a gun jabbed in their ribs and a hissed warning in their ear. George Kennedy was certainly the man to sink his teeth into the role and instils him with a genuine sense of danger and threat. Unfortunately Kramer seems to get bored very quickly with him. Cornelius finds gold in the river and quickly realises this could pay off all his debts. He could stop running and start living again, but after a quick song and dance from Sally, he happily tosses the rocks back into the water and throws himself into building a new irrigation system for the people of Shangri-La.

Neither Olivia Hussey nor Liv Ullmann ever seem happy with their decision to appear in the movie. Both look tense and ill at ease whenever singing and dancing is required. While Hussey copes okay with a restricted role, Ullmann had come from heavy, intense Ingmar Bergman roles to what is essentially a piece of fluff, and she never looks comfortable even in the non-singing sections. Ullmann constantly looks confused by what her role is and how she should be playing it. Eventually she chooses to just smile inanely while quietly praying that the whole thing will finish sooner rather than later.

Hussey, Ullmann and Finch were all dubbed in the film by Jerry Whitman, Andra Willis and Diana Lee respectively, but Sally Kellerman - to her eternal credit - decided to sing her own songs and it goes a long way to making her character the most likeable and enjoyable. Kellerman

is the only one who truly embraces both her role and the joy of the musical. She had a slight, reedy voice and virtually no ability as a dancer, but when the music starts she attacks each number with the verve and dynamism of a seasoned song and dance veteran and shows none of the self-consciousness of her colleagues. It's a shame her sense of joy and happiness didn't seep further into the fabric of the film. The character Harry Lovett has spent his life chasing after a dream of stardom that was always going to be out of reach and for Bobby Van it must have felt slightly biographical. Van had a genuinely good voice and could certainly cut it as far as dancing was concerned, but had never had the breaks to make the step from also ran to true star. *Lost Horizon* could have been Van's ticket to the big time and, although that didn't happen, it's more down to the poor songs and apathetic choreography than his lack of talent or enthusiasm which is second only to Kellerman.

If the cast came out if it reasonably unscathed, the same can't be said for Hunter. *Lost Horizon* would be the only film he produced at Columbia. After its failure, he moved to Paramount the following year and worked solely on TV movies. He died in 1996 having never produced another feature film. Oddly enough, despite the soundtrack being one the main weaknesses of the film, its release as an album was quite a success, and over the years many of the songs were covered by artists such as Fifth Dimension, Tony Bennett, Andy Williams, Diana Ross and even Elvis Costello. The film, which quickly became known as 'Lost Investment', was savaged by the critics on release. Vincent Canby called it "a big stale marshmallow." Pauline Kael, possibly the most influential of all critics, described Shangri-La as a "middle class geriatric Utopia." John Simon claimed the film must have turned up in garbage cans rather than film cans. Many years later, when asked if he would change anything in his life, Woody Allen replied: "No… except for seeing the musical version of *Lost Horizon*!" It also gave Bette Midler one of her most quoted wisecrack when she said: "I never miss a Liv Ullman musical!" In many ways, it's a genuine shame the film didn't turn out better and wasn't received more warmly by both critics and public, because beneath the unwieldy Kramer script there's quite a good story of positivity and optimism and a real sense that if we all tried to be a bit nicer and kinder the world would be a better place. As with many films that were shredded by the critics on release, *Lost Horizon* has gained a fairly loyal band of supporters (defenders if you like) who'll tell you that it isn't as bad as its reputation. It even has its own Facebook page for devotees to chat about the perceived merits of the film and to debunk some of the more acidic remarks that have been made down the years.

Watching *Lost Horizon* again just recently I came to two inevitable conclusions. First of all, as so many films have shown in the past (and I'm sure many more will show in the future), you can have some of the best names in their individual fields, but it's no guarantee that the ingredients are going to mix well and that the film is going to work. Secondly, back in 1973, 8-year-old me should have argued a hell of a lot harder to see *Live and Let Die* instead.

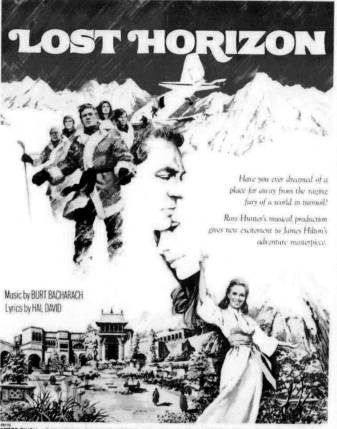

ADVENTURES...
OF A SECOND DIVISION SEX PEST

In the shadow of the later, smuttier _Carry On_ films and the _Confessions_ series with Robin Askwith, Ian Taylor takes a look at the _Adventures_ series (1976-1978).

Humour often travels awkwardly - across countries, across years, and also across movies. The chance of there being many film fans in America who are aware of the _Adventures_ movie trilogy that popped up (oo-er, missus!) between 1976 and 1978 is minimal. That any of them might be _fans_ of the series is unlikelier still. Not just because of the decidedly British humour, but also because of the contextual aspects. The socio-political references. The parade of well-known faces from stage, screen and light entertainment. The nostalgia for what things once were in the sceptred isle of their creation, for good or for bad.

True, this article could end up being a checklist of double entendres and sightings of greater and lesser spotted boobies. But those are only a couple of aspects which

make this short-lived series of sex comedies interesting. There's more to them than that.

Firstly, there is something that readers need to understand about the British film industry at that time. And it's not just that, like humour, the British way was often fundamentally different than the Hollywood way. No. To put it simply and brutally, the British film industry was on its arse during the '70s. The ongoing popularity of television (increasingly in colour), and the introduction of home video players, had seriously dented theatrical takings. Investment was at a low. Big players like EMI and Rank started the decade strongly but were on the ropes by the end of it. As the decade wore on, the only way

to garner a few quid seemed to be to release soft-core sex comedies or big screen spin-offs of popular television shows. That's why EMI's _Confessions of a Window Cleaner_ was the biggest hit of 1974. It's also why Hammer struck gold, not with Dracula or Frankenstein, but with a big-screen adaption of the popular TV sitcom _On the Buses_. Both titles bring us to another point for consideration. For most in the UK, the '70s was associated with a poor economy, high inflation, employment struggles and strikes. If anyone was going to the cinema at all, it was likely because they wanted to watch something which would cheer them up. Let's remember that, and put our

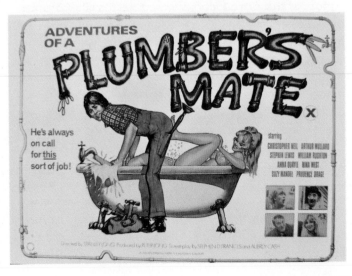

socially correct 21st century perspective to one side while examining these movies.

The laughs in British comedies from that era could legitimately be accused of being sexist and inherently racist. Viewers will also no doubt notice a peculiar contrast wherein the films seem to be ridiculing homosexuality one moment while worshipping the camp or gay celebrities as icons the next. Having made that clear, I don't intend to return to it much. Suffice to say, basic barrel levels were often scraped. Nevertheless, these movies still offer insights (sometimes witty, often depressing) into the socio-political climate of the time. Take *Carry On at Your Convenience* (1971), for example, which combines boozy office daytrips, romantic entanglements and embarrassments, saucy gags, toilet humour and an examination of staff unions and the economy!

Talking of *Carry On*, that particular movie series was beginning to flounder. It had evolved from generally genteel comedies into cheekier affairs in the late '60s. By the '70s, they found themselves descending into outright smut, thanks to looser censorship and a growing acceptance of nudity in cinema. More cheap, independent sex comedies appeared. The *Carry On* series never quite found the right balance and was superseded by the *Confessions* films, based upon books written by Timothy Lea, starring Robin Askwith as a likeable loser always trying his luck at a new job and with every passing dollybird. The first proved a big hit for EMI, and the floodgates truly opened. Yet it would ultimately prove to be a brief spurt (oof!) before the UK industry hit rock bottom.

Looking now, the films work as examples of low comedy (pratfalls and prodding), socio-political observations (a world of bowler-hatted businessmen of privilege are unable to service their neglected wives, so the wives turn to broad-accented working class blokes to get the job done) and an opportunity to see how we used to live (for all the ogling of bums and boobs, there is also the nostalgic sight of branches of Woolworths and the National Westminster Bank on busy high streets).

Most of these productions were abject, failing to amuse or titillate, remaining standalone releases. However, beyond *Carry On* and *Confessions,* there were another couple that manged to stretch to trilogies. One was the obscure 'Alan Street' trio of shorts starring physique model turned actor John Hamill (*Trog, The Beast in the Cellar, Tower of Evil*) that began with *Just One More Time* (1974) and was followed by *Girls Come First* (1975) and *Under the Bed* (1977). Hamill later reflected: "Those sex movies ruined my career. But you know how it is, I was out of work, the birds were smashing, and I've always been a born flasher!" His last regular acting work was on television, in the 1978 Doctor Who serial *The Ribos Operation* before he retired and turned to running a pine furniture shop.

The other trilogy is better known and was far more successful. The *Adventures* films might have been second division fare - operating on a fraction of the budget of their competitors, riffing off stuff that was already out there - but Columbia Pictures were happy with the results of their minor investment. *Adventures of a Taxi Driver* (1976), *Adventures of a Private Eye* (1977) and *Adventures of a Plumber's Mate* (1978) were box office successes in the UK, and were eventually sold globally to over 30 countries.

All three movies take their lead from the *Confessions* series, focusing on a cheeky chappie involved in a different trade with each passing tale.

The first *Adventure* stars Barry Evans as *Taxi Driver* Joe North, but he opted out of the sequels. Maybe this inspired the change of character, as Christopher Neil took over and played *Private Eye* Bob West. When Neil returned to play a *Plumber's Mate* in the third and final film, he was then named Sid South! It's a shame that there wasn't a fourth film to enable him to become Bill East!

Considering the similar basic concept of a working-class bloke on the job (*Adventures* had a taxi driver, a private eye and a plumber's mate, while *Confessions* had a window cleaner, a pop performer, a driving instructor and holiday camp employee), it's quite amusing to note the presence of a certain name on the writing credits of *Adventures of a Taxi Driver*. Suzanne Mercer (*Groupie Girl, On the Game, Naughty!*) may be acknowledged as the writer of the

screenplay, but this is addended with an additional note saying: 'From an idea by Stanley A. Long'. (This conjures up an image of dear old Stanley sitting at his desk, having a lightbulb moment wherein basically he says to himself: "I know! Let's rip off the *Confessions* films!")

For those unfamiliar with the name, Stanley Long (who directed and produced all three *Adventures* productions) was unequivocally a key player in UK independent films from the '50s to the '70s, and a towering colossus in the field of X-rated pictures. He started as an assistant at the 'Picture Post', photographing dancers in their skimpies at Soho's famous Windmill Theatre. It led to him forming Stag Films in 1958. This was to produce striptease/glamour photos and 8mm films, and business was booming. At 25, Long had produced his first cinema release, *Nudist Memories* (1961). Further titles included *Sex and the Other Woman* (1972), *On the Game* (1974) and *Eskimo Nell* (1975). But there was more to Stan than sex comedies. He was also a camera operator on Roman Polanski's brilliant psychological chiller *Repulsion* (1965), and he lent his skills as a cinematographer to Tony Tenser's Tigon for the horror films *The Sorcerers* (1967) and *The Blood Beast Terror* (1968), working for celebrated genre directors Michael Reeves and Vernon Sewell and with treasured horror stars Boris Karloff and Peter Cushing. It was the success of the *Adventures* trilogy though, that made millions for Long's distribution company Alpha Films, making it one of the most successful independent British distributors of the '70s.

One other thing to remember is that the combination of struggling film industry and the country suffering economically meant that these productions could attract a staggering amount of celebrity talent. The calibre of some of the names on the cast list is sometimes mind-boggling. This will become apparent, starting with *Adventures of a Taxi Driver* with Barry Evans playing the titular cabbie. His breakthrough was the lead in *Here We Go Round the Mulberry Bush* (1967) which led to television success in

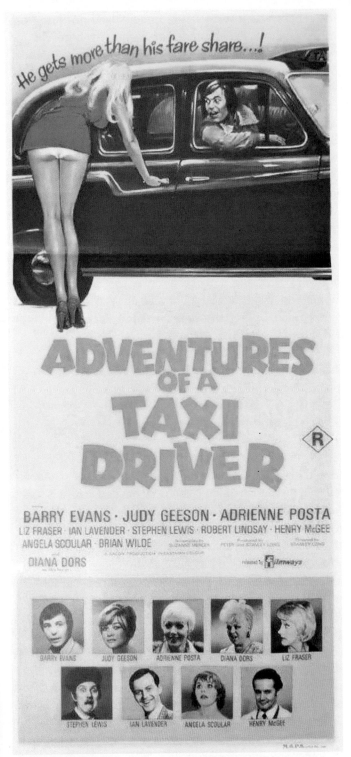

the series *Doctor in the House* (1969-70) and *Doctor at Large* (1971), inspired by Richard Gordon's novels and the big screen releases between 1954 and 1970. Long caught an episode and thought Evans ideal for the role of Joe North. Although variations of the *Doctors* sitcom continued throughout the '70s, Evans quit in 1971 to focus on theatre, but bills needed to be paid and he was lured back to star in the first *Adventures* film. In a way, this new role was not so different from his best-known work. Yes, there was a change of profession, but he was still an affable young bloke getting in trouble by flirting with girls. There was just a lot more nudity, and not just from actresses! Evans himself ended up flashing his buttocks and more, but Long remembers him being "very professional, even when I got him running down roads or climbing down ladders totally nude."

Evans was a good-looking fellow with an easy charm on camera, useful when breaking the fourth wall and talking to the audience about his shenanigans. There was a reunion of sorts with three actresses from *Mulberry Bush*: Judy Geeson, Adrienne Posta and Angela Scoular. The first two found their careers suddenly veering towards sex comedies concurrently, both making appearances in *Percy's Progress* and managing a *Carry On* film apiece before returning to more salubrious material. They managed to keep their clothes on, but Scoular performed gamely in a very revealing bath scene in which she sits atop a submerged Evans whilst hubby Brian Wilde (from TV's *Porridge* and *Last of the Summer Wine*) keeps bobbing in and out of the bathroom for a chat!

Basically, the script offers short sketches backed by jaunty music, intercut with stock footage of London sights and black cabs. The quality of dialogue is summed up by the likes of Geeson asking "Fancy a quick one before I go?" before brandishing a teacup and owning a python called Monty. Most comedic plusses come from Evans trying to retrieve his shirt from a naked Jane Hayden (yes, Linda's sister) while she argues with her husband Ian Lavender (of *Dad's Army*), or individual performers offering fun portrayals, such as Posta's faux posh voice and mispronunciations. Her delivery of "Do not put all your balls in one basket" is far more amusing than it has any right to be thanks to the way she says it. There is the expected procession of horny housewives of all shapes, sizes and ages (only their partner's neglect of them and a propensity for losing clothes linking them). Posh Mrs Devere-Barker (Prudence Drage) asks: "Be an angel, would you, and just slip it between my lips." To which Evans replies: "Oh, the *glass!*"

However, there is a darker side to it all. When Anna Bergman bares her wares as a stripper, it cuts to queasily lip-smacking men of all ages and types. It's rather sobering. Then there is British legend Diana Dors (once the smouldering beauty of *The Last Page* and *Tread Softly Stranger*) playing Evans' mother as a foul-mouthed, sour-faced matriarch in hairnet and overalls. To cap it all, there's a circular narrative

bookending the whole movie. Evans picks up a crying Jane Hayden (playing Linda, her more famous sister's name... coincidence?) Evans immediately looks into the camera with "I know what she needs, right?" before she asks to be taken to London Bridge where she intends to commit suicide. It's uneasy viewing, more so when the comedic cabbie uses it to get sex from her. The film ends with him picking her up again - this time she wants the Post Office Tower - and Evans rolls his eyes as if to say: "Here we go again." Worryingly, this seems almost uplifting!

Despite queasy morals throughout (Evans is engaged to Posta's character), the film was a success, perhaps due to further cameos from the likes of *Carry On*'s Liz Fraser (giving a blow job in the back of the taxi with disastrous consequences), Stephen Lewis (*On the Buses*), Robert Lindsay (*Get Some In, Citizen Smith*) and Henry McGee (*Benny Hill*).

Surprisingly, Evans turned down the sequel *Adventures of a Private Eye*, instead appearing in the flop *Under the*

aventuras de un detective privado

CHRISTOPHER NEIL · SUZY KENDALL · HARRY H. CORBETT
LIZ FRASER · ADRIENNE POSTA · IAN LAVENDER · DIANA DORS

DIRIGIDA POR   PRODUCIDA POR
STANLEY LONG · PETER · STANLEY LONG
GUION DE
MICHAEL ARMSTRONG · COLOR

live: milkmen in old-fashioned floats, for example, and another stunning list of familiar faces, including returns for Diana Dors, Ian Lavender, Liz Fraser, Angela Scoular and Adrienne Posta, alongside Harry H. Corbett (*Steptoe and Son*), Jon Pertwee (*Doctor Who, Worzel Gummidge*), Anna Quayle (*Up the Chastity Belt*), Willie Rushton (*That Was the Week That Was*), Robin Stewart (*Bless This House*), Shaw Taylor (*Police Five*) and Irene Handl (*For the Love of Ada*) as the implausibly named Miss Friggin. Veteran Fred Emney (*Fun at St Fanny's*) is rather hilarious in his last role playing a flustered rich gent in a dodgy club.

The script was written by Michael Armstrong (*The Haunted House of Horror* and *Mark of the Devil*) and he does a good job. The opening scene of a husband returning home from the night shift, climbing into the bed recently vacated by his naked wife and unwittingly putting his arm lovingly around Bob West's slumbering form is basic comedy. But it's well timed, with an amusing reaction from Neill as the hopeless apprentice private investigator and experienced lothario. He also manages a beautifully timed face-plant into an open grave at one point. Pertwee seems to be playing his rather grandiose real-life self as the proper P.I. who enjoys having a naked secretary.

Armstrong makes less of the working-class drudgery and casual cheating of the main character but maintains the slapstick and sex. However, he adds an old dark house sub-plot and a vague curse - "the bird from Hell"! It is therefore fitting that Euro Horror scream queen Suzy Kendall (*Assault, The Bird with the Crystal Plumage*) plays the female lead. She is perfect as an ex-model who introduces the spooky house/blackmail-via-pervy-photos plotline. Still, it was the last movie she made so she clearly wasn't impressed with the way her acting career was going!

Some surprising nudity arises when Posta, playing a singer/dancer, performs a cabaret routine then while getting changed lets one boob hang out. She later claimed this was an out-take and got lawyers involved until Long was able to prove this was not the case. A full-frontal sex scene in a punt features Linda Regan (later a regular in the sitcom *Hi-De-Hi*), and it has to be said she's built for it! A rowing team zip by with their cox shouting "in-out, in-out" while Neil's arse bobs up and down in time to the rhythm - it's indicative of much of the humour, I suppose. This is a better film than the first, as there is more of a story. But it loses marks for some regrettable blackface, when Neil poses as an Arab while trying to escape from regular horror support Milton Reid.

The final movie *Adventures of a Plumber's Mate* brings back Anna Quayle, Willie Rushton, Stephen Lewis (as a plumber named B.A. Crapper!) and posh totty Prudence Drage. It also adds Arthur Mullard as a gangster, Christopher Biggins as a man fixated on a female blow-up doll (!) and, surprisingly, Elaine Page (fully clothed) just before her musical career took off. Her lawyers ensured

Doctor before starting the long-running sitcom *Mind Your Language*. Stanley Long considered Richard O'Sullivan and Dennis Waterman as replacements, but settled on Christopher Neil, a musical performer who had worked on a bizarre variety of projects from sex comedies such as *The Sex Thief* to an educational series for under-fives called *You and Me*!

Neil was a decent, charismatic replacement, willing to make a fool of himself via slapstick and happy to flash his body parts now and again. His musical background saw him write and perform the theme tune for both films (later leaving acting to focus on music, actually producing the Sheena Easton Bond theme which featured in *For Your Eyes Only*!)

Again, there are great glimpses of how we used to

that Long couldn't use her new-found star power to advertise the film!

Unfortunately, this one slips back into the grotty home life setting - in this case an untidy bedsit with unpaid rent - and unpalatable misogyny. Times were clearly changing at pace as there is far more blatant simulated sex, complete with a battered pussy - actually a pet cat trapped under the bed!

There is an unusual McGuffin in that Neil unwittingly obtains a criminal's stash (gold which the bad guy has melted down into a toilet seat!) There are so many wide boys and wheelers-and-dealers in it that it feels like a pervy episode of *Minder* or *Only Fools and Horses*. In fact, thinking about it, all three in the series have elements of criminal activity as either main or sub-plot. This, at least, sets them apart from *Confessions*.

The smut is unevenly spread here, leaving the movie unbalanced, but the bondage woman, swingers party and tennis club shower sequence are memorable enough, if a little tawdry. It was clear it was near the end of the road for such material.

As pointed out, many of the contributors went on to better things or had hitherto enjoyed strong careers. There were two particular tragedies, however, which make for a sad coda. Barry Evans fell on hard times after a revival of *Mind Your Language* was cancelled in 1986, and actually ended up working as a taxi driver for real. In 1997, he was found dead in his home, surrounded by empty whiskey bottles and aspirin. His phone lines had been cut and credit cards stolen but there wasn't enough evidence to convict anybody of any crime. Even worse, Leslie Phillips' wife Angela Scoular, who had long had mental health issues, died in 2011 after ingesting acid drain cleaner and pouring it on her body, causing lethal burns to her digestive tract and skin. An inquest decided that she had killed herself while the balance of her mind was disturbed, and stated that her death was not suicide. Both sad ends for people who tried to cheer us up with their sauciness and cheekiness in the '70s.

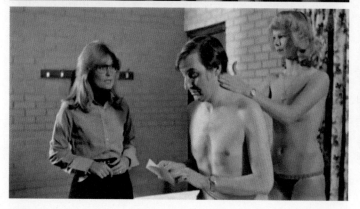

96

Original Artwork by the Students of Confetti Institute of Creative Technologies

Confetti is a specialist creative technology education provider in Nottingham, England, dealing in fimmaking and VFX, video game design and game art, music production and live performance. The following artwork is original work produced specially for this magazine by students aged 17-18 years.

Alien with Jonesy
by Ruth Hobbs

Star Wars
by Ben Alderman

STAR WARS

"You may fire, when ready"

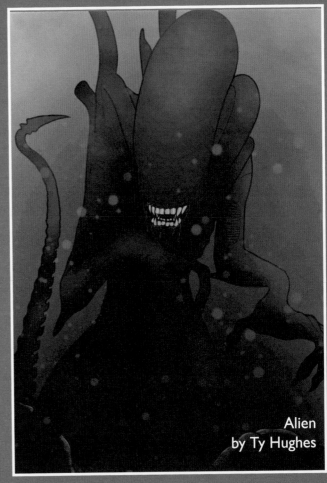

Alien
by Ty Hughes

The Godfather by Eva Gosling

CLOSING CREDITS

Simon J. Ballard

Simon lives in Oxford and works in its oldest building, a Saxon Tower. Whilst also working in the adjoining church, he has never felt tempted to re-enact scenes from *Taste the Blood of Dracula* or *Dracula A.D.1972*. He has never done this. Ever. He regularly contributes to the magazine 'We Belong Dead' and its various publications, and once read Edgar Allan Poe's 'The Black Cat' to a garden full of drunk young people at his local gay pub The Jolly Farmers. His first published work was a Top Tip in 'Viz' of which he is justifiably proud.

Rachel Bellwoar

Rachel is a writer for 'Comicon', 'Diabolique' magazine and 'Flickering Myth'. If she could have any director fim a biopic about her life it would be Aki Kaurismäki.

David Michael Brown

David is a British ex-pat living in Sydney. Working as a freelance writer he has contributed to 'The Big Issue', 'TV Week', 'GQ', 'Rolling Stone' and 'Empire Magazine Australia', where he was Senior Editor for almost eight years. He is presently writing a book on the film music of German electronic music pioneers Tangerine Dream and researching the work of Andy Warhol associate and indie filmmaker Paul Morrissey for a forthcoming project.

Sebastian Corbascio

Sebastian is a writer/director and novelist. He was born and raised in Oakland Ca., and lives in Copenhagen, Denmark. His motion picture work can be seen on Youtube/Sebastian Corbascio. His murder mystery novel 'Sarah Luger' can be found on amazon.com. Reach him at facebook.com Sebastian Corbascio

Martin Dallard

Fed on a staple diet of the *Six Million Dollar Man*, repeats of the Adam West *Batman* show and the likes of the *Flashing Blade*, and *Champion the Wonder Horse* from a young age, it's no wonder that Martin is self-confessed geek for all things '70s. And whatever you do, don't get him started on the likes of Ron Ely's Doc Savage, as you'll never hear the end of it. Whether it travelled in a TARDIS, or it rode in a red double decker bus, he watched it. But rest assured he never switched off his television set and went and did something less boring instead…

John H. Foote

John is a critic/film historian with thirty years experience. He has been a film critic on TV, radio, print criticism, newspaper and the web, for various sites including his own, Footeandfriendsonfilm.com. He spent ten years as Director of the Toronto Film School, where he taught Film History, and has written two books. The first was an exploration of the films directed by Clint Eastwood, the second a massive volume of the works of Steven Spielberg. Scorsese is next. John has interviewed everyone in film, except Jack Nicholson he quips. His obsession with film began at age 13.

John Harrison

John is a Melbourne, Australia-based freelance writer and film historian who has written for numerous genre publications, including 'Fatal Visions', 'Cult Movies', 'Is It Uncut?', 'Monster!' and 'Weng's Chop'. Harrison is also the author of the Headpress book 'Hip Pocket Sleaze: The Lurid World of Vintage Adult Paperbacks', has recorded audio commentaries for Kino Lorber, and composed the booklet essays for the Australian Blu-ray releases of *Thirst*, *Dead Kids* and *The Survivor*. 'Wildcat!', Harrison's book on the film and television career of former child evangelist Marjoe Gortner, was published by Bear Manor in 2020.

James Lecky

James is an actor, writer and occasional stand-up comedian who has had a lifelong obsession with cinema, beginning with his first visit to the Palace Cinema in Derry, (now long since gone) to see *Chitty Chitty Bang Bang* when he was six. Since then, he has happily wallowed in cinema of all kinds but has a particular fondness for Hammer movies, spaghetti westerns, Euro-crime and samurai films.

Darren Linder

Darren grew up in the '70s and has been forever enamored with films from that decade. He is a lifelong resident of Oregon, currently living in Portland. He has performed in many rock bands, ran a non-profit dog rescue, and worked in social service with at-risk youths. Currently he works security in music venues, and is completing a book about his experiences there to be published later this year. His favorite film directors of the '70s are Sam Peckinpah, Francis Ford Coppola and William Friedkin.

Kevin Nickelson

Kevin has been a fan of cinema of all genres and decades since age 4. As he grew older he found his passions for dissecting various aspects of film and decided to marry this obsession with his ability for creative writing into writing about film. Kevin has written for 'Scarlet the Magazine', the 'Van Helsing Confidential' and the site classic-horror.com. Currently, he writes for 'We Belong Dead' magazine and books, 'Scary Monsters' magazine, horrornews. net and will soon be working for 'Scream' magazine. Kevin is also co-host of the Grim and Bloody podcast produced by Death's Parade Film Fest.

Brian J. Robb

Brian is the 'New York Times' and 'Sunday Times' bestselling biographer of Leonardo Di Caprio, Keanu Reeves, Johnny Depp and Brad Pitt. He has also written books on silent cinema, the films of Philip K. Dick, horror director Wes Craven, classic comedy team Laurel and Hardy, the *Star Wars* movies, Superheroes, Gangsters, Walt Disney and the science fiction television series *Doctor Who* and *Star Trek*. His illustrated books include a History of Steampunk and an award-winning guide to J.R.R. Tolkien's Middle-earth. A former magazine and newspaper editor, he was co-founder of the Sci-Fi bulletin website and lives near Edinburgh.

Allen Rubinstein

Allen grew up in an upper-middle-class neighborhood in suburban Connecticut. He writes about movies and history and tries to reveal the truth wherever possible. He works with his wife on a teaching organization called The Poetry Salon (www. thepoetrysalon.com) in Costa Rica while taking care of far too many cats. He has not yet told his parents that he's an anarcho-syndicalist.

Peter Sawford

Peter was born in Essex in 1964 so considers himself a child of the '70s. A self-confessed film buff, he loves watching, reading about and talking about cinema. A frustrated writer his whole life, he's only recently started submitting what he writes to magazines. His favourite director is Alfred Hitchcock with Billy Wilder running him a close second. He still lives in Essex with his wife and works as an IT trainer and when not watching films he's normally panicking over who West Ham are playing next.

Joseph Secrett

Joseph is a film nut and collector who started at a young age, and quickly became infatuated with all things cinematic. He is a huge fan of 20th century cinema, especially the '60s and '70s for their sheer diversity of genres. Top choices of his include revisionist westerns and seedy crime dramas.

Ian Taylor

Ian dabbled in horror fiction in the early '90s before writing and editing music fanzines. He later adjudicated plays for the Greater Manchester Drama Federation but enjoys film analysis most. Over the last five years, he has become a regular writer and editorial team member for 'We Belong Dead' magazine and contributed to all their book releases. This has led to writing for Dez Skinn's 'Halls of Horror', Allan Bryce's 'Dark Side' and Hemlock's 'Fantastic Fifties', amongst others. His first solo book 'All Sorts of Things Might Happen: The Films of Jenny Agutter' was recently released as a 'We Belong Dead' publication.

Dr Andrew C. Webber

Dr W has been a Film, Media and English teacher and examiner for over 35 years and his passion for the cinema remains undiminished all these years later. As far as he is concerned, a platform is where you wait for the 08.16 to Victoria; dropping is something that louts do with litter; and streaming is how you might feel if you were in *Night of the Hunter* being hotly pursued by Robert Mitchum with "Hate" tattooed on his knuckles and Stanley Cortez doing the cinematography.

Steven West

Steven's first published work was as a floppy haired teenager, voice breaking as he scribbled about Terence Fisher for an early issue of 'We Belong Dead' - a useful break from the lingerie section of the Freeman's catalogue. He still writes for the magazine and its spin offs while regularly contributing to 'The Fantastic Fifties' magazine and the UK Frightfest website, alongside www.horrorscreamsvideovault. co.uk. In 2019, Auteur Publishing released his 'Devil's Advocate' book about Wes Craven's *Scream*. Steven lives in Norfolk with his partner, daughter and - thanks to permanent home working - a dozen sock-puppet 'friends'.

Printed in Great Britain
by Amazon